Always an Angel

Playing the Game with Fire and Faith

Tim Salmon with Rob Goldman

TRIUMPH
BOOKS

To Marci

Copyright © 2010 by Tim Salmon and Rob Goldman

No part of this publication may be reproduced, stored in a retrieval system, or transmitted in any form by any means, electronic, mechanical, photocopying, or otherwise, without the prior written permission of the publisher, Triumph Books, 542 South Dearborn Street, Suite 750, Chicago, Illinois 60605.

Triumph Books and colophon are registered trademarks of Random House, Inc.

Library of Congress Cataloging-in-Publication Data

Salmon, Tim, 1968–
  Always an Angel : playing the game with fire and faith / Tim Salmon with Rob Goldman.
    p. cm.
  ISBN 978-1-60078-343-2
  1. Salmon, Tim, 1968– 2. Baseball players—United States—Biography. 3. Los Angeles Angels of Anaheim (Baseball team). I. Goldman, Rob. II. Title.
  GV865.S185A3 2010
  796.357092—dc22
  [B]
                                    2009048978

This book is available in quantity at special discounts for your group or organization. For further information, contact:
  Triumph Books
  542 South Dearborn Street
  Suite 750
  Chicago, Illinois 60605
  (312) 939–3330
  Fax (312) 663–3557
  www.triumphbooks.com

Printed in U.S.A.
ISBN: 978-1-60078-343-2
Design by Patricia Frey
All photos courtesy of the Angels unless otherwise noted

Preface

I first met Tim Salmon in Tempe in 2004, while I was collecting interviews for my first book, *Once They Were Angels: A History of the Team*. Tim Mead, Angels vice president of communications, had granted me an hour in the clubhouse, and Salmon was high on my hit list. Upon entering, I beelined to his locker and was immediately struck by his accessibility, sincerity, and intelligence. He seemed genuinely glad to share his opinions, which were frankly stated and articulated without cliché. I walked away from our 10-minute interview thoroughly impressed.

That brief encounter with Tim stuck in my head. A few years later, when it became time to pen another book, I thought his time with the Angels would make for a compelling story. If he would expand his thoughts about baseball and include something about his personal life, we could really be on to something.

I brought the book concept to Tim and he was all for it. A series of extensive interviews followed, and after writing them up I sent them on to my talented editor, Pete Ehrmann, in West Allis, Wisconsin. As with any book, the process was slow and agonizing. But two years later I finally presented the final edits to Tim.

I wasn't prepared for what came next. Tim wanted the final manuscript to be in his own words. I warned him that a wholesale rewrite of it would be time-consuming and a lot work, but Tim insisted that the book be in his own voice. As with everything else he's ever done, he wants his fans and future grandchildren to remember him on his own terms.

Tim tackled the challenge head-on. He ripped my draft apart and reconstructed it into something all his own. I'll never forget the night he began emailing me his final draft, chapter by chapter. Staring at my computer screen, I was awestruck. He had revamped the entire manuscript, telling his story in his own words and cadences. *Not bad,* I thought, *for a former right fielder who left college after his junior year.*

Just as I did, you are about to discover that Tim is not just a talented athlete but also a gifted and perceptive writer. From his troubled youth to a glory-filled October night in 2002 when his late-game heroics single-handedly kept his team's hopes alive in the World Series, Tim brings it all back in vivid fashion.

Tim's story is, in effect, the Angels' story. His career mirrors the Angels' dramatic rise from a modest-market team to one of baseball's golden franchises. From the late 1980s through today, Tim shares with us the ups and downs of the Angels and all of the personalities and struggles in between. This book is not just the personal memoir of a key member of the Los Angeles Angels but also an insider's history of a crucial period in the team's development.

I sure didn't expect to end up sitting on the bench for my own book, but when you've got one of the Angels all-time greats on the field—or at the keyboard—you give him his freedom. It could not have worked out any better for me and for the fans of Tim and the Angels. I have no doubt they will all be thrilled by what follows.

—R.G.
Thousand Oaks, California
October 2009

Introduction

When I joined the Angels in 1992, the club was basically a mom-and-pop organization owned and operated exclusively by Gene and Jackie Autry. The Autrys loved their ballclub, and the team had an established history of luring big-time free agents out West to play for the Singing Cowboy. But after years of struggling to win the big one and successive losing seasons, the Autrys grew weary. The passing of Mr. Autry in 1998, combined with rising salaries and operational costs, contributed to Jackie's decision to sell the club.

By the time I left the team in 2006, 14 years and two owners later, the Angels had morphed from a small-market club into a major-market franchise with a World Series trophy and a winning reputation. From the Autrys' humble stewardship to Disney's glitz and glitter to Arte Moreno's marketing genius, my time with the club was a memorable ride. Starting in my rookie season of 1993, the team began building a homegrown nucleus of talent that would be the foundation for its first world championship.

When I retired from the game, I was content to fade away into normalcy and do the things that most fathers do with their children. No more road trips to keep me away from recitals and Little League games. Now I can volunteer all of my time and contribute to everything my kids are involved in. I often get asked if I miss the game. At first my answer was an emphatic *no*, but each year that passes seems to soften my stance. The Angels have invited me to participate as a guest coach in spring training during the last few years. It has surprised me how much fun it is to pass along insight to the next wave of Angels players. More than anything, I think it is slowly kindling my passion to be around the game more in the future. Writing this book has stoked the fire a little as well. As I look back on my journey to the big leagues, I realize there were so many people and experiences that played a part in my success. I have come to realize now that fans are interested in hearing about them as well. No matter how many people read this book, writing it was well worth it. And I know four kids who will be happy to someday read it to their own children.

When compiling the stories for this book, it wasn't individual accomplishments or experiences that came to mind so much as it was the marvelous array of teammates—the colorful personalities and people who helped mold me into the big-leaguer I became. A former teammate of mine, Shawn Boskie, once said, "Someday when you look back on the game and reflect on your teammates and friends, you won't remember the stats or their individual accomplishments, but more important, their personalities and the relationships you had with them." This book is a memoir of sorts, a historical journal and collection of tales that also paralleled the creation of the modern-day Angels. My desire is to share some of the positive insight and experiences about my life and my big-league career. It is intended to be a fun and easy read. There won't be any startling revelations or sensational accusations, as has become popular in this day and age. I always had the utmost respect for the game and the players who took the field, and that won't ever change.

When I look back on my career, one word describes it best: *perseverance.* Every big-league player has had his own trials and tribulations to overcome along his journey. I have always approached mine as a

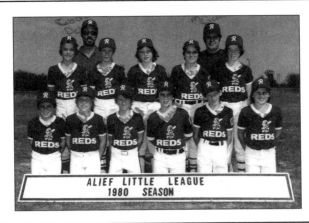

Here I am (front row, far right), in Wichita Falls, Texas. Photo courtesy of the author

In the picture, my messy hair made me look like Kelly Leak, the wild kid in the movie *The Bad News Bears*. I wasn't happy about it at the time, but now when I look at that picture I'm proud of the kid who had the initiative and determination to be there for his team photo.

But for all the pressure playing sports brought, the necessity of constant planning and adaptation to circumstances also had an upside. It forced me to organize my thinking, and this focus made me very self-reliant. I became a perfectionist, always striving to prove myself to everyone. In every new school, I had to show a different group of kids that I belonged. It played a huge part in who I am today.

Through all this there was an important influence in my life. Thanks to my grandmother, I grew up with a simple faith in God and His protection for me. I would go to church with her whenever we visited her and even attended catechism classes because of her influence. I can remember the times when she would tuck me into bed and teach me how to say the Lord's Prayer. She always reassured me that whatever situation I faced in life, my Father in Heaven was there looking down on me and protecting me. As a young boy I came to rely on this assurance all the time.

Now, I realize this is supposed to be a baseball book with baseball stories, but I feel this is an opportune time to share some of my personal beliefs. I believe that every person has a set of core values that establishes a foundation for dealing with life.

I have always strived to be a man of integrity and character. There is no better compliment I could receive than to have parents tell me they are thankful for the role model I have been to their kids. The values I have strived to live by are not by my own doing; rather, they are the principles taught by Jesus Christ in the Bible. These principles have become a template that has helped guide my decision-making.

The foundation for this belief was established by my grandmother, but it was further nurtured when I went away to college. When I received a scholarship to Grand Canyon College, I knew I was going to a good baseball program. What I didn't know was that it was a Christian school affiliated with the Southern Baptist church.

During freshman registration, I found out that I would be taking Bible classes and attending chapel twice a week. Being a formative time in my life, the Bible took on new meaning and from it, I developed a new understanding of God and his purpose in my life. At the same time, I became good friends with a senior on the team named Acey Martin. Acey took me under his wing and showed me how to play the college game of baseball. Off the field, he was a great mentor, too. He gave me insight into the Biblical teachings I was learning about in my classes. It was through this friendship that I came to understand why I needed to have a personal relationship with Jesus Christ. My decision to commit my life to Christ took place in the second semester of my freshman year.

My life on and off the field slowly began to reflect the lessons talked about in the Bible. Looking back, I think the biggest change was the way I perceived the world around me. God had a plan for my life and wanted me to seek Him in all that I did. I began to look and see how God was using circumstances to mold me. The greatest change came in the way I approached the game. "Playing for an audience of one" is a phrase that Christians often use. That audience of one is Jesus, of course, not yourself, the fans, teammates, coaches, or even money. The focus is on using our God-given talents to the best of our ability and for the glory of God. To me, that meant pouring my heart into the game and leaving the results to Him. There is a Biblical verse that says "The horse is made ready for battle, but victory rests in the hands of the Lord." Years later, Mike Scioscia's mantra of, "one pitch at a time" had familiar ring to it, which made it easy to embrace.

Having a new perspective on my success and failure gave me a humility that always kept me grounded. Many times I was just as amazed as everyone at my success, knowing that it was all God working through me. Conversely, I was able to deal with my failures in a positive way, knowing that God was using it to teach me something. I can't imagine dealing with the stress and public scrutiny you get at times in the big leagues without Christ. Yet I realize most ballplayers do just that.

Being a Christian doesn't mean life will be successful or prosperous. It is not some kind of good luck charm, either. My life has been filled with good things, for sure, but I have also dealt with many difficulties along the way. My relationship with Christ has given me inner peace during those difficult times, knowing that God is still in control.

When I look back on my life, I can see God at work. I can see that the difficult circumstances I encountered as youngster were used to mold me into the man I am today. Trials like getting beaned in the face taught me valuable lessons about overcoming fear. The hardships my brother and I endured taught us lifelong lessons about self-determination and perseverance. Through it all I have always maintained a faith that my Father in Heaven is looking after me. I am so thankful to have had a grandmother that was committed to sharing the eternal hope we have in our God in heaven.

The Things That Mattered Most

It was football, not baseball, that was my real passion as a kid. I probably had a bit more natural ability in baseball, but I absolutely loved the gridiron. When we lived in the Dallas–Fort Worth area, I became a huge fan of the Dallas Cowboys and star quarterback Roger Staubach. One Christmas I got an official NFL leather football from my parents. I was about 12 years old. It was tough to get my small fingers around the ball then. I had trouble throwing it. Between that and Mike's trouble catching it, that ball got worn really fast, bouncing around on the cement. "Don't let the ball hit the ground," I'd scream at Mike, as if it were all his fault. "You're getting scratches on it!" Afraid of getting punched by me for dropping the ball, Mike forced himself to haul in even my most errant throws. Over time, his hand-eye coordination developed to the point where he had no problem handling everything I threw. Years later he played in the secondary for USC and the San Francisco 49ers, and he credited those early years on the street for his great hand eye coordination.

Mike and I moved out to Phoenix, Arizona, to live with my dad about the time I was entering high school. It was there that we finally established some semblance of roots, not moving again until we graduated from high school. Having newfound stability really contributed to my peace of mind, as well as to my production as an athlete. For the first time we weren't the new kids on the team. My two sports were football and baseball. Depending on the season, you could always find a football or baseball in my hands.

I was always on the slender side compared to most of the boys my age. Being a skinny kid, I had to work twice as hard in the weight room just to keep up. The extra work paid off, though, and by my junior year, puberty kicked in and I put on some muscle. I developed into a decent football and baseball player and realized for the first time that I might have some options after graduation. Borrowing a line from Bo Jackson, I guess baseball was always just a hobby for me; football was always where my passion was. But it was in baseball that my skills really shined. During that period I made some summer all-star teams and we won state titles, so it should have been obvious to me which sport was going to take me the furthest.

Still, I couldn't shake football. I had developed into a pretty decent wide receiver and even won outstanding receiver awards at ASU and BYU summer football camps. My goal was to play college football, but after my senior season, no scholarship offers had come my way. Those new developments made playing baseball an easy decision. At the time I wasn't thrilled about giving up football but it turned out to be a wise decision. Nonetheless, football helped shape the baseball player I would become. Getting back up after a hard hit and pushing myself to the limit proved useful in my future baseball experiences. I transferred the hard-nosed mentality I developed on the gridiron to the baseball diamond.

After my senior season of baseball I was offered a scholarship to play at a small NAIA college in Phoenix. Its baseball program had a great reputation for player development and hard-nosed baseball. At the same time, the Atlanta Braves selected me in the 17th round of the Major League free-agent draft. I was offered $15,000 to sign but decided against it. Years later I found out that I would have been a part of the incoming class of Braves players that included Tom Glavine, Jeff Blauser, and Dave Justice. Who knows? Maybe I would have won a World Series with the Braves.

Natural talent aside, baseball at Grand Canyon College wasn't easy. Our coaches demanded a nose-to-the-grindstone work ethic from us. They drummed into us the concept of working harder than our opponent. As an NAIA school, GCC didn't have any rules that limited our time on the field. We would play 30 or 40 games in the fall and close to 60 in the season with only two weeks off over Christmas. Attending classes was only a necessary requirement, as we were on the field by 1:00 and off no earlier than 6:00 every day. "The Canyon way" paid off, though. We were the No. 1– or No. 2–ranked team in the country in all three years when I was there. Twice we went to the College World Series, coming up just short of a championship both times. Grand Canyon had a no-non-sense, no-hoopla type of program. It was the perfect environment for me to really develop my God-given base-ball skills. This style of play laid the foundation for the way I would approach my pro-fessional career.

It was also at Grand Canyon that I developed my

My two years at Grand Canyon College were an incredible learning experience. It was there that I honed my playing skills—and caught the eyes of big-league scouts.
Photo courtesy of the author

low-key personality. My work and play on the field did the talking for me. The no-nonsense approach was constantly reinforced. We were reminded to get our heads out of the stands and focus on the game between the lines. It's obvious how this helped me when I got in the big leagues. There are plenty of things in the stands vying to distract you. In college, it was all about getting the distractions out of my way and to be laser focused on the job at hand.

Grand Canyon College provided the structure and character building foundations I'd been yearning for. There was only one more thing I needed too fully round out my life: a good Christian girlfriend. As it turned out, she was sitting right next to me in class. Because freshman English was overbooked, two classes were formed at the last minute. Sitting in a packed classroom with my baseball buddies, we scoped out the room for any girls who might make English more interesting. As the professor called out a list of names to move to the newly formed class down the hall, we all moaned in frustration when the captain of the pom squad, Marci Hustead, was summoned. After all the names were called, he asked for a couple volunteers to switch to the new class. Before he could finish the sentence, I was out of my seat and heading for the door. When I got to the new classroom, fate was in my favor: the only open seat was right behind Marci's. Shortly thereafter, we were asked to choose a partner for a poetry unit. When Marci turned around and asked if I had a partner, it began a relationship that would last forever. We married three years later and have brought four children into this world: Callie, Jacob, Katelyn, and Ryan.

Marci has been with me from day one of my baseball journey. Coming from a baseball family herself, she was always in the stands when I played. She has been much more than just my biggest fan, though. Part psychologist and part coach, she has given me counsel throughout the roller coaster ride of emotions that I experienced to get to the big leagues. With Marci I have more than just a wife; I have a partner in life.

Along with my grandmother, Marci is the most gracious person I've ever met. And she is very much like my grandmother in that she is grounded by her faith. Always looking at the world through God's eyes, she has taught me a lot about compassion and forgiveness. She has softened my rough edges, changing me from the self-reliant person I once was to a more nurturing and caring person. To use an example, growing up I never apologized to anyone for anything, because nobody ever apologized to me. When Mike and I played catch with the football and I threw it so it hurt him, it never occurred to me to say I was sorry. Tough guys didn't do that. If somebody hurt your feelings, you didn't ask for an apology. You zinged it right back, only harder. Marci helped me see things from a different perspective. If I said something that hurt her, she wanted me to acknowledge it and apologize for it. That took some getting used to. In the first few years of our marriage, telling her "I'm sorry" was the hardest thing for me to do. It was simply a character trait I hadn't developed as a kid. Years later, I even had teammates who commented about my lack of sensitivity. Thankfully, Marci has helped me change for the better.

Reeling in the Fish: Joe Maddon

One of the most unique relationships I forged during my career in professional baseball is the one I have with Joe Maddon. Joe is currently the manager of the resurgent Tampa Bay Rays, and the influence that he has had on that organization has been profound. So too was his influence on my career. Being the baseball intellectual that he is, many ballplayers have benefited from his instruction over the years. "Mr. Positive," Joe is probably the most optimistic person in baseball. In his world, the cup is always half-full.

Joe was also one of the first people to recognize my potential as a professional ballplayer. Our relationship began so early in my career that many jokingly called him my daddy. Joe was always one of my biggest supporters, and I was truly blessed when our lives intersected way back during my days at Grand Canyon College.

The first time I met Joe was at my dinner table, a few days after the 1989 amateur draft. Joe was a minor league coordinator for the Angels, and he did some local scouting in Arizona as well. Working in conjunction with the area scout, Tim Kelly, Joe had been scouting me at Grand Canyon College throughout my career. The first time Joe ever saw me play, I hit a couple home runs to dead center. That convinced him to start keeping tabs. During my junior season there were a ton of scouts attending our games who represented just about all the professional baseball teams. Although I might have met Joe during this time, I cannot really recall. There were so many scouts around that the names all seemed to blur, but I do remember that the Angels were not among the teams making serious overtures. Joe would tell me later that, based on the organization's needs at the time, I wasn't really on their radar. Nonetheless, he always kept tabs on me because I was in his own backyard.

On the day of the draft I was projected to go late in the first round. During the previous summer I had played in the Cape Cod League and made the postseason all-star team. Known as the premier collegiate summer league, the Cape distinguished itself by being a wooden-bat league. Scouts flocked from all over the country to watch the top college talent play in the league that best resembled professional baseball. Many of the players on that all-star team were projected top picks, and I was among them. I still remember all of the scouts' predictions; a few of them told me outright that I would be their first pick. Others said that if I somehow made it to the second round I would be theirs. Unlike today's draft, which is televised and

Through his nurturing and guidance, Joe Maddon helped mold the core of young Angels who would go on to win the team's first world championship.

covered by the media, there was nothing I could do but sit at home and wait for that phone to ring.

That day turned out to be one of the worst days in my professional career. All of my hopes were dashed when I didn't get a call that first day. The phone rang once. It was a local newspaper reporter checking in to see if I had heard anything. When I said no, the reporter remarked that it was odd, because they had already gone through the first three rounds. My world was shattered!

I finally got a call three days later from Joe Maddon telling me I was the Angels' third-round selection. I didn't know what I was more surprised by: the fact that I dropped to the third round or that it was the California Angels that drafted me. I immediately pulled out all the business cards I'd gotten from scouts. I didn't find any from the Angels. I could not get over the fact that all those scouts who said I would be their first pick had *three* chances at me and passed. It felt like *The Twilight Zone*. Welcome to professional baseball!

I came to find out from Joe afterward that the only reason the Angels drafted me was because I was the best player on the board when their turn came in the third round. They couldn't believe I was still there. They were very excited to get a player like me that late in the draft. The reason I was contacted three days later was due to a miscommunication with the local scout, Tim Kelly. Kelly was sick at the time of the draft, so the Angels brought in Joe to make contact and try to sign me. A few days later Joe came to my house to meet with my dad and me and to begin negotiations. He brought along Bruce "Jeter" Hines, another organizational coach. I would get to know them both very well over the next few years in the minor leagues. (In fact, all of the young players who came up to the big club during my career were influenced greatly by these two men.)

At the dinner table, after some small talk, Joe asked us what it would take to sign me. This was my first negotiation. A friend, who would later become my agent, had given me advice beforehand. He told me, "Whatever you do, don't give them a number. Don't short-change yourself by giving them a ceiling." It seemed to be the same strategy Joe took as well, and we spent a lot of time spinning our wheels bantering back and forth. Finally, out of frustration, my dad blurted out "$100,000!" And there it was. The ice was broken.

I could tell by Joe's expression that this was an extreme reach. Back in 1989, first-round bonus babies could command anywhere from $100,000 to $200,000. Thinking I was going to be a first-rounder, most of the discussion among family had been in this range. Unfortunately, I wasn't a first rounder; I went in the third round. We had no idea what the bonus range was for this round. In fact, I was prepared for the possibility of returning to Grand Canyon for my senior year. It was my only leverage, though I believe Joe knew that the Angels were lucky to get me as late as they did. I thought I was worth more than a typical third-rounder because I had some real first-round potential. Joe countered to our offer by saying the Angels were prepared to offer me $30,000. After further negotiations and a phone call to Bobby Fontaine, the Angels scouting director, Joe upped the offer to $45,000. We needed some time to think about and so we decided to call it a night and continue negotiations over the phone in the coming days. Joe mentioned that mini-camp was just a few days away and that if I was to break with the short-season team going to Bend, Oregon, I would need to be signed and at the workout. Looking back now, I should have called his bluff, but being so green to negotiations, his ploy worked.

Joe called a couple days later and we went back and forth until we came to an agreement: a signing bonus of $65,000 and the rest of my schooling paid for. All in all, it amounted to about $75,000 to $80,000, a far cry from the six-figure number we had expected just a few weeks before. But I was happy to be realizing my dream of professional baseball and thankful it was with an organization that felt fortunate to have me.

chapter 2

Realizing the Professional Dream

Minor League Uncertainties

Shortly after the June amateur draft in 1989, the Angels held a mini-camp for newly drafted players at Gene Autry Park in Mesa, Arizona. I remember walking into the minor league spring training facility for the first time. The color red is something that I vividly remember associating with the Angels from the very beginning, from the big "A" logo down to the red spikes everyone wore. I had that giddy feeling I remember having as a kid on Christmas morning. I had worn only white or black spikes up until that point, so those red shoes really stood out to me as something special.

It wasn't the big leagues yet, but there was an awe factor knowing I was now connected with a major league team. Putting that uniform on for the first time was so exciting and I couldn't wait to get outside and play. As I looked around the locker room, everyone looked like a major-league player wearing their new duds. I was finally realizing my dream of playing professional baseball. It didn't matter that I was a million miles away from actually playing in Anaheim.

As a kid, I dreamed about what it would be like to play in the major leagues. What I never imagined was what the road to there

We never dreamed our love for sports would one day take us so far. Here, my brother Mike wears his USC uniform and I am in my first Angels uniform. Photo courtesy of the author

would look like. The minor league system was a totally foreign concept to me. I didn't understand the different classification levels— Class A, Double A, Triple A—and what it took to play at each level. The movie *Bull Durham* provided my only understanding of the minors, which wasn't saying much. I felt like a new recruit into the Army: wide-eyed and very green!

Aside from adjusting to a completely new environment, I had trouble sizing myself up against the other players. Everyone there had some sort of talent, obviously, and dressed in those flashy Angels uniforms, they all looked like major league stars. Taking right field that first day with four other players, I remember thinking, *Wow, all these guys are just like me—trying to get to the big leagues.* Until that point, I was always the best player on the field. It was the first time I was around players that were all my equal. It was evident everywhere I looked.

Some were raw, straight out of high school; some were polished collegiate stars; and there were also recruits from Latin America. Those Latin guys were all pretty skinny, but man, could they throw! There were two of them in my group in right field during our first practice and I was embarrassed by my pitiful arm in comparison to theirs.

Then there was the language barrier. I had never been around players with whom I couldn't communicate. I have to admit, it is pretty intimidating working next to someone not knowing if they are laughing with you or at you. Looking back on my career, it is my biggest disappointment to have not taken more time to understand and speak Spanish. It was all too easy to expect them to learn English, not the other way around.

I was fortunate to start my career in the Angels organization. The Angels had also drafted a few of my college teammates, so I had some built-in familiarity in an otherwise new situation. Chad Curtis, Paul Swingle, John Marchese, Brett Merriman, Don Vidmar, and Matt Hyde—my fellow Grand Canyon compatriots—all became pretty good players for the Angels in the minor leagues.

It was an exhilarating time in my life. Playing baseball—and getting paid for it!—was a dream come true. Years later when I would go back to Gene Autry Park for B-squad games, a flood of memories always rushed back, reminding me of those first days in an Angels uniform.

Beginnings in Bend

Bend Oregon, Class A ball, Summer 1989

After I finished mini-camp, I was sent to the Angels' Single A affiliate in Bend, Oregon. I took a jet from Phoenix to Portland, and then hopped aboard a little two-prop puddle-jumper for the flight to Bend. A few other new players were at the airport when I got there, and as we stepped into our rickety old team bus I couldn't help thinking of *Bull Durham* again. Only instead of "Durham Bulls" on the side of the bus, it said "Bend Bucks" with a cartoon picture of a deer, Bucky Buck. The bus was a real relic, and all I could think was, *Oh my gosh, we're going to be living on this thing all summer.*

When we arrived in June, it was still cool in Oregon (unlike Arizona). Stepping off the bus late that night, I could actually see my breath. I remember the smell of pine trees in the air and thinking, *Where am I, on top of a mountain?* "Okay, this is where it starts," I said to myself. "This is the beginning of my professional career." I grabbed my bags and equipment and shuffled into the warm confines of my first minor league clubhouse.

The clubhouse was small, much like the one we had in college. It had an office for the manager, a small training room, a storage closet for bats, and a bathroom with showers, just the basic necessities. As I walked out of the clubhouse and into the dugout, I saw the field for the first time. It looked so pristine and calm under the moonlight, though I knew that in a few days it would be bustling with excitement. The mere thought of this started the butterflies in my stomach.

We had a few days of workouts and time to get settled in. I hooked up with my college teammate Paul Swingle, a pitcher I met in the Cape the year before named Erik Bennett, and shortstop Brian Specyalski. The four of us shared a two-bedroom apartment on the cheap side of town. There was the typical beer-in-the-fridge, wrestling-matches-on-the-living-room-floor, late-night kind of craziness you'd expect from guys who were away from home for the first time. It seems like I lived on peanut butter and jelly sandwiches. Then again, a salary of $650 a month doesn't buy much more than that. But I didn't go hungry. I was playing professional baseball. Besides, humble beginnings help build character and make you strive for something better. Not to mention, you can appreciate success more when it finally comes along.

What I remember most about that first season in Bend is not the actual playing time but my relentless insecurities. Even though I was one of the highest-drafted players on the roster and labeled a prospect, many of my teammates performed so much better than I did. My slow start at the plate had me concerned. I wondered if I had come to the end of the road in my career. As it turned out, I was worried for nothing. Little did I know at the time, the higher picks like me were the ones the organization had a strong vested interest in nurturing along slowly. The rest of the team was comprised of fillers and longshots. It was those players who had to produce early or be replaced immediately with the next wave of talent. The organization concentrated more on developing the high draftees, and if one or two of the other guys materialized into major league material, that was gravy for the them. "Survival of the fittest" is the best way to summarize life in the minor leagues. Having the right manager or scout behind you is as important as anything you can do on the field. With that stamp of approval, you'll stick around—and you might just get that call every minor league player dreams about.

As the season went on, I came to the realization that pro ball is a business. A lot of the time, there seemed to me no rhyme or reason to the personnel moves within the organization. Regardless of their performance, players were shipped in and out on a weekly basis. Some players became pretty good detectives, or so they thought, investigating the rationale behind every move. It seemed that the mind-set of the players wasn't about winning, but about putting up impressive individual statistics that would get them promoted to the next level. Self-promotion was prevalent. Guys complained about other players' good fortune. On several occasions, I saw guys' jealousy detract from their play on the field.

For me, it was all an education. I had no clue how the minor leagues operated or how players were moved through the system. I've been characterized as little bit naïve, but in this case, it wasn't such a bad thing. My philosophy was to always to perform to the best of my ability, make the most of my opportunities, and leave the rest to God. As it happened, it was the best thing I could have done. Throughout my career I was never promoted in mid-season—at any level. I went step by step, learned what I needed to learn, and moved on in the next season. By taking things one day at a time, I developed a solid foundation at every level in which I played. By the time I reached the big leagues, I was ready for anything that came my way.

The stadium in Bend was not built in a very well-thought-out location. The field was oriented so that when the sun set, it was directly behind the pitcher. This was pure hell for the hitter. During evening games, during the first three innings we were more concerned about not getting hit by a pitch than actually hitting the ball. Well, wouldn't you know it, I was the first casualty. Two months into the season we were playing an independent team from Boise and a pitcher named Steve King was on the mound. He was one of the more experienced pitchers in the league, as were many of the players on that team. Quickly behind in the count 0–2, the next pitch was meant to move me off the plate. I never saw it leave his hand. The glare consumed my vision and I stood there like a deer in headlights. Fortunately it was just a glancing blow, but the damage was done. The ball struck my face and broke my nose. I remember a few of the guys on the team really being upset at the pitcher for throwing high and tight in such blinding conditions. But that's baseball in the dog-eat-dog minor leagues. What else would you expect from a guy playing on an independent team, trying to make a living?

My first year of professional ball was over after that episode. I had surgery on my face, and believe it or not, they put a little cast on my nose. Everyone at home was of course concerned. But after they were assured that I was okay, the next question was, *What would I look like for my wedding in a few months?* As it turned out, I was just fine. I looked as good as new. But *my* next concern was how I would respond to the next pitch I would see. I had to wait until Instructional League in the fall to find out.

Maddon's Boys

Instructional League, Mesa, Arizona, Fall 1989

If there is a single melting pot from which the successful Angels teams of the early 21st century emerged, it is the fall Instructional teams in Mesa, Arizona. Instructional League is an extension of the summer season, where top prospects could continue their development under the guidance of the organization's instructors. The league was in Arizona, which took advantage of the spring training facilities and the fact that there were the other teams in the area. The Angels would bring in about 30 young players coming off a year of Class A or Double A ball to Gene Autry Park, often referred to as "the GAP." There, under the leadership of talented baseball men like Joe Maddon, Bruce Hines, Chuck Hernandez, Frank Reberger, and Bob Clear, the seeds of future Angels championship teams were sown. I'm talking about players like Garret Anderson, Jimmy Edmonds, Damion Easley, Gary DiSarcina, Troy Percival, Chad Curtis, Darin Erstad, and myself.

The seeds were sown on that very first day of Instructional League. Joe Maddon gathered everyone on the infield field grass before our first workout and announced, "You guys have got to believe you're going to be that next generation of players to help this organization win its first championship!" We were all young and raw, and we believed every word he said. Okay, let's just say we might have been a *little* skeptical. The big leagues still seemed a million miles away. It was the late '80s and "the Bash Brothers" from the Bay Area, the Athletics' Jose Canseco and Mark McGwire, were dismantling the league. As I looked around, I didn't see anyone on the team who had the physical size or even the skill that was on display out there in Oakland. Still, an interesting thing happened that fall that gave us a glimmer of hope.

In 1989, the Bay Area experienced one of our worst natural disasters when a violent earthquake shook the city so severely that daily life came to a stop. It happened right before the start of Game 3 of the World Series between the San Francisco Giants and the Oakland Athletics. Some joked that it was the A's bat bag falling off the equipment truck. I remember seeing the news accounts of the players streaming onto the field in Candlestick Park looking for their families in the stands to make sure they were all right.

Because of the earthquake, the World Series was postponed until the city got back on its feet. Both the Giants and the A's made the decision to come back to their spring training facilities in Arizona to stay sharp and continue workouts. For us in the Instructional League, it was weird to have the two teams in town. When word got back to us that select players from the A's Instructional League team would be involved in intersquad games with the big club, it hit home with us young players. We knew and played against those guys in the A's Instructional League, and there they were, taking the same field as the big leaguers—and in some cases having success. Putting it in that perspective helped us realize we weren't too far removed from being that caliber of a player.

For me at least, the dream became a little more real. Hearing Joe Maddon and the rest of the Instructional staff tell us it was within our power to make baseball history for the Angels organization didn't seem like such a long shot. We were in training to become champions. That's the mind-set they were constantly promoting. "Approach this like you are the first stones being laid," Maddon repeatedly said. "We're building a foundation of success for this organization, and you're going to be the ones that take that success and put us on the map." The coaches instilled in us a philosophy that you hear about in the Dodgers and Yankees camps. The Angels lacked that special identity that comes from winning championships, and from day one that's what Maddon and his coaches wanted to create with us. I can still remember Joe saying, "You are the core, the ones who will bring the Angels their first championship." They probably fed that line to every Instructional League team that came through then and today, but it couldn't have fallen on more receptive ears than ours.

Throughout that whole fall, they hammered into us just who our competition was and that we should start preparing for them now. Our Instructional League included teams from the Oakland A's and Seattle Mariners organizations, their major-league counterparts being in the same division as the Angels. When we'd play them, we were reminded, "You're playing against the Oakland A's today. These same players are going to be in the major leagues and playing against you someday. Let's start our dominance today. Start beating them right now, so that when we get to the big leagues they're used to getting beat by you. Set the tone for who we are today!"

My Instructional League class that first fall included Chad Curtis, Damion Easley, Jimmy Edmonds, and Troy Percival. The following year brought a sweet-swinging young pup named Garret Anderson. Instructional League is often called "Destructional League" by many of its players. And it was a lot like boot camp; everything you think you know about the game is broken down and retaught. Those were long days, and to beat the Arizona heat, we were often on the field between 7:00 and 8:00 AM. Extra hitting, extra fielding, extra base running, extra throwing, extra meetings…there was always something. My feet hurt and my hands ached after every practice. And then when we started playing games, my self-esteem took the biggest hit. It was a huge adjustment in my game, trying to apply the new techniques and skills I was learning.

One experience still occasionally haunts me in my sleep. A contingent of major league coaches and scouts from the big club had come down to evaluate some of the organization's younger talent, much like Mike Scioscia does with his staff today. When I arrived at the park I was informed that I needed to be dressed for early batting practice. Walking on to the field to hit, I realized it wasn't a run-of-the-mill extra batting practice. Doug Rader and Deron Johnson, the Angels' major league manager and hitting coach were leaning on the cage ready to watch me swing away, along with some other team staff. It might sound like a golden opportunity for me to show off my stuff, but I was terrified. I might have welcomed it at another time, but at the moment I was struggling with some major mechanical issues in my swing. Looking back, they might have gotten wind of this and made the suggestion to get me out there so that they could help figure it out.

At any rate, the hitting session went something like this: *swing, step out, try this, step in, swing, no that didn't work, try this, nope… Ah, there's no hope. Take it to the showers!* At least that was my impression. I wish I could say it was a great experience, but it wasn't. I was so distraught afterward that I thought about quitting altogether. If you had handed me a bat, I wouldn't have known which end to hold, I was so confused. It ended up being a great lesson, though. It taught me that I really needed to know who to trust when it came to messing with my hitting—or any part of my game, for that matter. Everyone has an opinion, and often other people's intentions are good but can be counterproductive. Sometimes you need to let it go in one ear and out the other.

Instructional League was all about building a foundation for the way things were going to be done in the organization. It had to be done because players were brought in from all different backgrounds and experiences. There I was, a kid out of college—and, in some cases, two or three years older than the kids who were straight out of high school or Latin America. Some were in dire need of training and discipline because it was the first time they had ever been away from home. It wasn't just about teaching the kids how to play professional baseball but also about how the professional player goes about things on and off the field.

One of the early disciplines they taught us was taking care of our equipment, particularly our shoes. Every morning before we started our stretch, we were called to the baseline and directed to stand at attention for our shoeshine check. Frank Reberger, the minor league pitching coordinator, conducted it. He had a little bit of Monty Python–meets–*Hogan's Heroes* in him. He'd walk up and down the line like a drill sergeant, barking out our names and questioning our ability to shine shoes. "Are those shoes shined, soldier?" he'd demand. "Yes sir," we'd belt out, only to have him reach down and swipe his long, crusty index finger across them to check for himself. Frank's antics always incited roars of laughter from the guys. Shoeshine checks were so much fun and a great way to break up the monotony of the long days. As difficult as it was to go through the learning curve of retooling your game, Instructional League was still a lot of fun at times. Some of my best memories and relationships are from those dry, hot days in Arizona.

Percy's Switch to Pitch

Instructional League, 1990

Instructional League was always full of new experiences, which kept it fun. One particular activity was always a hit with the catchers and outfielders, and in one instance, it changed the life of a player and the

Former catcher turned pitcher, Troy Percival

fortunes of the organization. Every year Chuck Hernandez, the minor league pitching coordinator, held a pitching clinic for the position players. The goal was to help the catchers and outfielders understand the proper throwing mechanics (and also to build arm strength). These were obviously tools that would need to be developed before advancing to the next level.

It was really fun. He taught us about using our legs for proper balance when throwing, the arm slot of the elbow, and the release point. At the end of the session, we took our turns throwing off a pitcher's mound so that we could understand the concept of balance and throwing downhill. The best part of it all was throwing in front of a radar gun. I had never measured my arm strength that way before and I always wondered how hard I could throw. One by one, we all took our turn trying to best each other's speed marks on the gun. My max effort approached 90 miles per hour a few times, but that was nothing compared to one of our catchers.

Troy Percival, then on the roster as a catcher, turned out to have some pretty decent stuff. "Percy" was a very good catcher, and he had a cannon behind the plate. But his downfall was that he couldn't hit to save his life. On the mound, they discovered he consistently threw in the low- to mid-90s. The Angels knew that he had some experience as a pitcher in college before they drafted him. He ended up becoming one of Hernandez's special projects. Chuck had Percy throwing in the bullpen next to the outfield where we ran our drills. We'd see them and yell, "Chuck, he's a catcher!" Not for long, though. Chuck knew what he was doing. The rest is history.

I was there to witness the creation of a great pitcher and a year later Chuck Hernandez thought he might get his claws into another one. I was really struggling at the plate, and I found out later that Chuck lobbied hard to get me into his bullpen laboratory. Fortunately I had guys like Joe Maddon who believed that my assets would be more valuable elsewhere. Whenever I see Chuck Hernandez nowadays he says, "You know, Fish, I'm glad we stuck it out as a hitter. You did pretty well!"

A Beaning in the Sun

Class A, Palm Springs, 1990

When I made the decision to play baseball over football, everyone lauded my choice, saying that football was a riskier sport where injuries were concerned. Of course, no one imagined what lay ahead for me after I signed with the Angels. I was beaned in the face by a pitch during my first season in Bend. And if that wasn't enough, I was the lucky recipient of another beaning the very next season.

It happened playing Single A ball in Palm Springs, California. Anyone who has ever been to Palm Springs knows that the sun is everywhere—even in the shade. It gets so hot there in the summer that you feel like you're playing baseball on the surface of the sun. Unfortunately, I can't blame the sun again for this second beaning; that one was all on me.

Prior to joining the professional ranks, I hadn't seen many sliders at all. Most guys like me learn to hit the fastball and maybe a curveball, so reality hits pretty hard the first time you see a slider. As a matter of fact, this is usually the end of the road for most aspiring hitters. A slider is a hard curveball. The curve action is small and much tighter. It comes out of the pitcher's hand in a fastball slot, which makes it hard to distinguish from a fastball, but this pitch travels slower. It seemed like every pitcher I faced in Single A was throwing them. Everybody from the peanut vendor to the batboy had advice on how to hit them—"Stay on it longer!" "Don't pull off!"—but nothing helped. I got so lost and confused at the plate that I really thought I had met my match. My career was over unless I figured out how to hit this pitch.

One of the things I had learned over time is that pitchers usually don't throw fastballs for strikes when the count is in their favor. Instead, they'll waste a pitch or throw one high and tight to move you off the plate. This, of course, sets up the pitch they *really* want to get you out with: the slider. On that fateful day in Palm Springs, I hadn't learned all this yet. Unfortunately I never got to the slider. I was down 1–2 when San Bernadino's Kerry Woodson threw one up and in on me, intending to brush me off the plate. With two strikes in the count, I was so fixated on trying to hit the slider that I just leaned over the plate a little too long. And like a heat-seeking missile, that inside fastball chased me down. At the moment my brain sent the message to turn my head, the ball exploded in my face. It didn't hurt right away, but when blood and broken teeth started gushing from my mouth and the catcher started moaning, "Oh my God! Oh my God!" I figured, *This cannot be good.* I tried working my jaw but it wouldn't budge. There was something lodged under my tongue, (It turned out to be broken teeth.) The trainer came running out with a handful of towels to stop the bleeding and led me off the field. I remember the expressions on my teammates' faces as I passed the dugout. They looked at me like I had just sprouted a third eye and horns.

The horrified looks continued in the clubhouse as I was ushered on to the training table. The only exception was my wife, Marci, who had driven in town that weekend from Phoenix to watch the game. When she walked in, she didn't even bat an eye. From her cool reaction, you would have thought that I'd been hit by a Wiffle ball. I couldn't really talk, so I motioned for a mirror to see for myself. I couldn't believe what I saw. My lower face was swollen, my lip was mangled, and I had a bloody mess of teeth and gums in places they shouldn't have been. The ambulance came shortly thereafter and they rushed me to the hospital.

As soon as word got out, my family started to arrive at the hospital. My brother Mike drove in from Phoenix, and it's amazing he didn't end up in the hospital himself. Driving like a maniac through the night, he fell asleep at the wheel and drove into a ditch. Luckily, he escaped serious injury and made his way to the hospital. When Mike walked into the room, he was shocked to see what kind of shape I was in—though tubes and needles probably made me look worse than I was. Mike later recalled that it looked like a hand grenade had exploded in my mouth.

I had a large suction cup over my damaged mouth that whisked away saliva and fluids that made a gurgling sound when I breathed. My jaw was broken on the left side and my chin was shattered into several pieces. The doctor compared my chin to a light bulb in a sock that had been crushed. My bottom front teeth were wedged under my tongue on impact. I needed surgery to reconstruct my jaw, but because my electrolytes were out of whack from the heat during the game, I had to wait three days before they could finally operate. I lay in the hospital on a morphine drip writing notes to my wife and any visitors who stopped by. My Uncle Daryl from Riverside brought the family over to see me, and I will never forget the get-well gift they brought me: a giant Jawbreaker! I was too drugged up to see the humor in it at the time, but looking back, that was pretty funny.

The doctors wired my jaw shut and did a good job of molding my chin back together. I lost four teeth, and numerous others needed root canals to anchor the permanent bridge I would eventually get. I was completely restricted to a liquid diet for the next six weeks. Back then there weren't the meal replacement drinks that we have today. Anything and everything that could fit in a blender was pureed into a mashed-potato consistency. The bonus to losing four teeth was the gap it created in the front of my mouth. I used a large plastic syringe to squirt blended food into my mouth through the gap of missing teeth. This tactic really helped me keep my weight up. I lost only 10 pounds during that period.

When I was finally cleared to leave the hospital, Marci came to drive me back home to Phoenix. On our way out of town, she stopped at In–N-Out to get some lunch for the drive across the desert. I hadn't eaten anything substantial for like four or five days. At the drive up window, she handed me the food to hold while she drove. I now know how a dog feels when its master feasts on a steak in front of it. The smell of that burger and fries drove me crazy. Finally, I couldn't take it any longer, so I grabbed a French fry and threaded it through the gap from my missing teeth. *Ahh…there it was…on my tongue!* Then I realized, *What do I do now?* I couldn't chew it, so I just sucked on it for the next 20 miles until it finally dissolved.

Spending my summer back home in Phoenix gave me a lot of time to reflect on my life and my career in baseball. For the longest time, I kept reliving the event over and over in my dreams—and each time I still couldn't get out of the way. I often woke up in a cold sweat, my emotions running high, wondering if I had played my last baseball game. I remember thinking, *All right, God, if you're telling me not to play baseball anymore, there has to be an easier way to get the message across.* As a Christian, I believe that everything happens for a reason. Every experience gives us an opportunity to build on our faith in God. We may not always understand it initially, but that's where having faith in God's goodness and His plan for us all is the key. I realized during this time that I wasn't in control of my career. It was His to give to me or take away. When we truly believe that God is in control of our lives, then that means all areas of our lives. I came away from the experience realizing that I was holding on too tight to my baseball dream. It was God's will to bless me or to move me through another door. I remembered a verse out of the Bible, Proverbs 3:5-6: "Trust in the Lord with all your heart, lean not on your own understanding. In all your ways acknowledge Him, and He will direct your paths." For me to heal both physically and mentally, I knew that I needed to put aside my desires and trust in Him completely for my next step.

The nightmares slowly subsided. When I returned to the game, I was anxious to get in the box and face live pitching again. For precautionary reasons, I wore a plastic shield on my helmet that extended from the ear pad and over my jaw. I really didn't mind it, but I noticed that it affected the way pitchers threw to me. To those who respected the injury, trying to pitch away from me actually had the unintentional, opposite effect at times. Others who didn't care about the injury tried to use it to their advantage, bringing more inside fastballs. Regardless, I knew at some point that I would need to do away with the guard and just take my chances.

Looking back on that experience, I remember that there were many people who supported me through a difficult time. I cannot say enough about my coaches and teammates who all rallied behind me. Bill Bavasi, the Angels' minor-league director, really put me at ease from an organizational standpoint. He let me know that the team would do whatever it took to get me through it and get me back on the field. I remember being sent to Las Vegas to work out with the Triple A team in Edmonton at the same time that Devon White, Jack Howell, and Bobby Rose were all there. Being around those major leaguers really helped stoke the fire in my heart to play baseball again. There were other things that helped, too. Joe Maddon contacted Dickie Thon, a former Angel who had once been hit in the face and had suffered injuries similar to mine. Dickie sent me a thoughtful and encouraging get-back-on-the-horse letter that meant a lot to me. A few years later I ran into Dickie in Double A and had the opportunity to thank him personally.

When I look back on my career there are so many great memories. I have a greater appreciation for them because I know how close I was to not having any of them at all. My faith in God and the lessons I learned growing up were refined through these early injuries. Ultimately, these experiences shaped me into the person I am today and paved the way for the player I became in the big leagues.

chapter 3

Working Up the Ladder

Fernandomania, Texas Style

Double A, Midland, 1991

In 1991 I broke spring training with the Double A club in Midland, Texas. It was my first big jump, and it got me out of Single A ball for good. Class A is characterized as a league for young players, and Double A was filled with more veterans and experienced players. It was a promotion for which I might not have been completely ready, but it was a welcome change from the hard-throwing pitchers who hadn't quite learned to control their stuff. One of the best things about Double A was occasionally playing against or with former major leaguers. In 1991, after Fernando Valenzuela had been released by the Dodgers and was pitching down in Mexico somewhere, the Angels signed him as a free agent. The plan was to have him throw a couple games in Midland and Edmonton before bringing him up to the big club. As a former Dodgers fan, I was ecstatic.

I wasn't the only one excited. Suddenly the entire Texas League was in the grip of "Fernandomania." Valenzuela's first game with us was in Little Rock, Arkansas, and the stadium was jam-packed. It was standing room only that night. The outfield was roped off, allowing fans to sit on lawn chairs along the warning track and in foul territory. There was so much electricity in the air that it seemed like a World Series game. I had never been so nervous at the start of a game. It seemed like we were playing in the big leagues. It was electric. I'll never forget it. Neither will I ever forget that bus ride home after the game. Even though alcohol was officially off-limits, Fernando sneaked a case of Coronas on board. From the back of the bus, he discreetly doled out the bottles, making sure to keep them hidden from our manager.

It didn't take long for us to realize that Fernando's presence on the team could be good for everybody. Back in Midland, his presence on the field could actually help some of us pad our wallets. It was typical, in a lot of minor league towns, that every time the local team hit a home run, the fans would pass a can around the stands for donations to that player. After an inning or two of making its way around, the player who hit the home run would find the cash sitting in his locker after the game. With Fernando pitching for us at home a week later and bringing in a huge crowd, everyone had his prediction of what that home-run windfall would be. *Someone's going to make 500 bucks*, I thought to myself. Considering I was making only $850 a month, that was hardly chump change. Guys talked about it for five straight days. It was every man for himself. "We're all swinging for the fences when we get back to Midland," was our rallying cry.

On the day Fernando finally pitched in Midland, the fans were lined along the warning track and in foul territory just as they had been in Little Rock. Under normal circumstances, a home run was anything that went over the rope holding back the spectators. We didn't even have to clear the fence—*ka-ching*! Well, in the third inning, I did it. It was one of the few times in my life I actually hit a home run when I was trying to do so. As I circled the bases with more than my usual enthusiasm I couldn't help but think to myself, *They're going to be passing around that can for four or five innings.*

No sooner had I sat down on the bench and soaked up the congratulations of my teammates that my mental calculations were rudely interrupted. Damion Easley stepped up to the plate after me and proceeded to hit his own home run. *Now what? How are they going to differentiate my money from his? Mine was first, so that money going into the can belongs to me. Doesn't it?* Damion had his own idea about that, of course. After we sat there for a while arguing like a couple of IRS bean counters, Easley suggested that we split the proceeds. I wasn't happy about that, but being good friends, I relented. When the precious can was emptied in the locker room after the game, we shared in a $600 payday. The next day Marci and I celebrated our good fortune. We put on our dress clothes and ate high on the hog at the Golden Corral that night.

That whole year in Double A was a lot of fun. Playing alongside Fernando and some other big-leaguers I had grown up watching made me realize that they weren't all that different than the rest of us. Maybe, just maybe, big-time baseball was closer than I thought.

Minor League Player of the Year

In 1992, after coming off a full season at Double A, I had my first opportunity to attend a major league spring training camp. This was back in the day when the team split time between Gene Autry Park in Mesa, Arizona, and in Palm Springs, California. For the first half of the spring we played all away games in Phoenix and then in about mid-March we headed to Palm Springs. I knew that it would only last a few weeks but nonetheless I was excited to be there.

Unlike the way spring training is run today under the Scioscia regime, back then young players like me rarely saw any action in the

"A" games. If there were any "B" games to play, they were done on the backfields away from any of the excitement attached to the big club. I was only around long enough to see maybe a dozen games from the bench and I can recall vividly my one and only at-bat. Playing the Oakland A's at Phoenix Municipal Stadium, I had one of those typical late-inning at-bats. You know the kind: most of the stars are out of the game and the fans have left. Still, it had a big-league feel to me. I flew out to left field on a hanging curve. Nothing special, but at least I got myself in the official box score the next day. There I was, in the same box with Jose Canseco and Mark McGwire. It was pretty cool.

As short as my stint was, it was a big confidence boost for my game. My everyday catch partner was Lance Parrish. There's something about being around guys like that. They are true professionals and I started to feel like a big leaguer. I was able to familiarize myself with the players, coaches, trainers, and other Angels personnel. Having that familiarity would help me later if I was called up.

After a few weeks of camp, I was part of the first wave of players who were sent down to finish up spring in the minor leagues. I was assigned to the Triple A Edmonton club, at least temporarily. Unbeknownst to me, the organization had me slotted to return to Double A Midland to start the season. They were just waiting for the big club to finalize its roster so they could slot the rest of guys sent down. I had a very up and down season the year before, and the staff thought it would be good for me to tighten up my game before promoting me. I wouldn't have disagreed at all, so I was a little surprised to see myself on the Edmonton roster. My newfound confidence carried over into my game that spring. I was playing pretty well, and when an unexpected move occurred with the big club, I didn't get bumped down to Double A. They let me start out the season in Edmonton, but on a very short leash.

The Edmonton team was made up of veteran players who either had major league service time or were on the bubble. Being around all that experience proved to be beneficial. I learned a lot about the game by observing the way these guys prepared themselves. In addition, the coaches had a different approach to things than those at the lower levels. Max Oliveras, "Mako," was the manager and his approach was very much like that of a major-league manager. Guys at this level pretty much knew how to play the game so there wasn't so much of the babysitting you might see elsewhere. We were treated like men, and if we didn't perform, we were probably going to be sent down. That level of expectation changed my approach to the game. I hadn't been in that situation since college, where I felt the pressure to perform or be benched.

Lenny Sakata, the former infielder for the Baltimore Orioles, was another coach on staff who was quite helpful. He was great, and he balanced out some of Mako's roughness for us younger guys. He was also a great hitting coach. Unlike most of the other coaches who tried to straighten out the mechanics of my swing, Lenny focused more on the mental side of hitting. Rather than talk about pulling off the pitch, he asked questions like, "What pitch were you looking for?" "Did you notice the pattern he is setting?" "You need to look off-speed against this guy." I had spent the last three years overhauling my swing so much that I forgot about the dynamic between the hitter and the pitcher. Crazy as it seems, this is often the case with minor-league players. Having Lenny around really helped me get over the hump.

We opened the season in Edmonton, and hitting down in the lineup I banged out a couple hits. In the next game I got a couple more, and the next a few more. The hits just kept coming. I was just as surprised as everyone else by my early success. I couldn't put my finger on the transformation in my game, so I kept a guarded confidence. I put the blinders on, put my nose to the grindstone, and didn't stop to ask questions or reflect on my success. As it turned out, I was learning an approach to the game in a way that I applied throughout the rest of my career. Sure, it would have been nice to be able to stop and smell the roses sometimes, but it just didn't work that way for me. I felt like I was always teetering on the brink of returning to my old ways, which were full of so much frustration. I told myself to stay focused and stick to the game plan. Ultimately, it was my fear of losing momentum that turned my game around.

Looking back on my experience in Triple A, I know that it was there that I learned to be patient at the plate and how to hit the off-speed pitch. Toward the end of the previous season in Double A Midland, I had an eye-opening conversation with my outfield coach, Gene Richards. He wasn't a hitting coach, but he left me with a few words of wisdom about hitting. He observed firsthand my erratic season of multiple batting stances and struggles with off-speed pitches. I was too coachable, he told me. In an effort to find my game and please everyone, I listened to *too much* advice. He told me, "You need to know your swing better than anyone else." Those words hit me right between the eyes. He was right. I had no idea what my swing was. It lacked a foundation. I tried anything.

In baseball, there are no quick fixes. There is a learning curve in most things and the foundation you build on will dictate how long it takes to make the adjustment. For instance, when I was learning to hit off-speed pitches I made it more difficult by always changing my stance, hand position, or approach. Rather than focus on one thing at a time, I had too many variables in the mix. All of those moving parts complicated things once the pitch was released. I took Gene's words to heart. It took me an off-season of committing myself to one setup in the box and sticking with it. Ultimately it was *my* career, I decided, and I had to start taking responsibility for it. If someone had some advice for me, it needed to fit into the scheme I was working from, otherwise it would go in one ear and out the other.

It turned out to be a bit of a perfect storm in 1992. I had my batting revelation, the confidence boost of big-league camp, added pressure to perform, and a coach like Lenny to get me thinking on the right track. It was all coming together in a big way. With my swing finally in the proper groove, by the All-Star break I was pushing triple-crown numbers. The Angels were having a rotten season in California and my teammates were laying bets that I would be a mid-season call-up. I didn't give it much thought, though. I was finally happy to be having success and honestly, I didn't want to do anything to disrupt it.

The summer passed without a call. The organization was thinking the same thing I was: *Let him finish out the year and feel good about his accomplishment.* And then the call finally came on August 22, a week before the Triple A season ended. I narrowly missed the triple crown—by four percentage points in batting average—and was named Minor League Player of the Year. The Angels made the right decision. That award put me on the big-league radar, and it was like a "Get Out of Jail Free" card. Now, even if I struggled a little bit the following year in the majors, people might cut me some slack because I was the Minor League Player of the Year.

Baptism in the Bronx

Yankee Stadium, August 20, 1992

Traveling in the minor leagues can be tough. As a player, you endure long, all-night bus rides and early-morning wakeup calls when you finally get to fly. It can be even tougher on the wives. In Edmonton, we flew to most of the cities we played in, but our wives would have to pile in a car and make the trips on their own. It was one such trip to Calgary where Marci arrived just before game time only to find that I wasn't in the lineup. I had some good news and bad news for her. Mako informed me just before game time that I would not be playing that night because the big club had purchased my contract. I got the call! I was headed for the big leagues! It was very exciting news for the Marci and me, but I was disappointed to tell her she would not be going with me. Marci had followed my career from the early days at Grand Canyon College. Brought up in baseball, she had been in the stands for the majority of those contests. Getting to the big leagues was a call-up for both of us, really. But she couldn't go; instead, she had to make her way back to Edmonton and pack up our things. So with our new puppy in tow, Marci had to move our things back to the States and I went to New York.

After an early wake-up call the next morning, I boarded a jet headed for New York via Toronto. My stomach was tied up in knots with anxiety. *Would I make it in time for the game? Would I be in the lineup?* Typically, if you were called up, you were slotted to play that night. I couldn't get over the fact that by the time I would lay my head on my pillow that night, I would have played in the big leagues! It was so amazing to be realizing my childhood dream.

My instructions were to grab a cab at the airport and head straight to Yankee Stadium. My flight arrived at about 4:30 PM, just in time for the afternoon rush hour. After a day of flying across the country, being stuck in traffic was the last place I wanted to be. Sitting in traffic, that close to realizing my dream was excruciating. When I finally arrived, the taxi dropped me off right in front of the stadium entrance. There I stood with two big equipment bags and no idea where to go next. When fans streaming into the stadium realized that I was a new player, they began to shout, "Who are you? "You somebody special? Sign this for me?" Getting into the clubhouse was quickly becoming difficult. Then out of nowhere some burly cop came over and asked me suspiciously, "Are you a new player? Follow me." I was passed off to another cop, who escorted me downstairs to the clubhouse.

The first person I saw was equipment manager Leonard Garcia. He shook my hand, congratulating me, and handed me a uniform. "Hurry up and get dressed," he said. "Maybe you can get some swings in before batting practice is over." I tossed my stuff in my locker and started putting on my gear when interim manager John Wathan came by and told me to meet him in his office as soon as I was dressed. John became the manager late in the year after the Angels team had a terrible bus accident. On an East Coast swing, the team was en route from New York to Baltimore when the bus driver fell asleep. Manager Buck Rodgers and a few of the players suffered injuries that shortened the season for them. John was serving as the bench coach at the time, so when Buck couldn't get back on the field, John took over as interim manager. The ship was already sunk for that season and the team was trying to finish it out on any positive note when I joined them.

I stood in front of John's desk. "Great year, Tim. Congratulations," he said. "I know you were hitting cleanup all year, and that's great. You did what you needed to do down there, and I have you hitting cleanup tonight." He quickly added, "No need to put any pressure on yourself. Our cleanup hitters are batting a combined .160 this year, so anything you can do will improve upon that. Now get down on the field there and get in some swings."

Thanks to my good friend, rookie Chad Curtis, I managed to get in five or six batting practice swings before the game. Chad knew I had been called up and was waiting for the word of my arrival. Waiting at my locker when I came out of John's office, Chad quickly ushered me down to the field. After batting practice, I was reintroduced to Tim Mead, the team's public relations person. "Congratulations and welcome to the club. If you have a couple minutes, could you address our media? They've been expecting you all year and would like to talk to you," he said. All of a sudden I had about 15 reporters surrounding me. Probably only half of them really knew who I was, but in New York, the media travel in a herd. In the minors I occasionally gave interviews but never to a crowd like this. As they fired questions to me about my background and expectations, my head swam. I can only cringe thinking about what might have come out of my mouth.

After 20 minutes of "meet the press," I hustled my way back to the clubhouse to change out of my practice uniform and get a quick bite to eat before returning to the field for the 6:40 pre-game stretch. My stomach was churning like a garbage disposal when the game started. But as soon as I stepped into the on-deck circle to await my first major league at-bat, all my nerves instantly disappeared. When I put the weighted donut on my bat and started taking some swings to get loose, a sense of peace came over me. I had done this before. Sure, the venues were much different, but the game was the same. It made me think of the movie *Hoosiers*, when Gene Hackman's character takes his team onto the court before the state championship game. He takes out a tape measure and has his boys measure the court and rim. It was a great moment in the movie, teaching the valuable lesson that the only thing that changes is the crowd. The game is still the same.

So as I walked to the plate for my first big league at-bat, it was no different than in Calgary the night before. My emotions in check, I approached it like any other at-bat during that season. My first big-league pitch from Shawn Hillegas was a fastball right down the middle for a strike. Under the bright lights of Yankee Stadium, the pitch looked as fat as a pumpkin. *I can hit that all day*, I thought to myself. The next pitch was another fastball just off the plate outside. "Strike two," exclaimed the umpire. I was a little surprised by the call, but I didn't show any reaction. I automatically kicked into my two-strike approach. Calm and collected, I went from being down 0–2 to laying off four straight balls to work a walk. Making my way down the first-base line, I caught sight of the Yankees' first baseman. *Holy cow! There's Don Mattingly!* After a brief congratulations, it was back to the game. But there I was, standing next "Donnie Baseball." I'll admit, it was a thrill.

In the bottom of the first inning, Mattingly hit a long fly ball in my direction. I thought I had a good bead on it, but as I reached the right field warning track and leaped, my shoulder hit the wall. I got my glove up barely over the fence, but because I got caught on the wall, the ball glanced off the tip of my glove and over the fence for a home run. The crowed erupted as the Yankees star rounded the bases. All I could think to myself was, *I almost stole a home run away from Don Mattingly*. Those thoughts were quickly interrupted when the famous "Bleacher Creatures" rudely brought me back to earth. In New York, the fans in the cheap seats beyond the right field fence are notorious for their lack of etiquette. Much like the student section of a college football game, they are the most inebriated and boisterous fans in the stadium. Throughout entire game they cheer for the Yankees and say every rotten thing they could think of to the right fielder. That happened to be me that night. I was barely in the outfield five minutes before they were screaming at me, "Hey, skinny, you can't play with these men!" I think that was the only printable line they gave me. They also had a chant they'd yell over and over to the annoying cowbell beat: "Yankee baseball! Mets suck! Angels suck! Salmon sucks! Marci sucks! Everybody sucks!" I was so impressed that they already knew my wife's name. The media had nothing on the Bleacher Creatures. They came prepared.

We ended up winning the game 9–5. After my first at-bat walk, I struck out twice, lined out to left, and grounded out to short. Soaking in the win from the clubhouse afterward, Chad Curtis informed me we wouldn't be taking the team bus back to the hotel. Instead we were going to take advantage of our celebrity status and make some money. We were going to meet and sign autographs for a bunch of people in George Steinbrenner's luxury box along with two other players, Greg Myers and Rob Ducey. We'd get paid $1,000 apiece for the first hour and $500 for every 30 minutes after that. Two hours later, Chad and I left Yankee Stadium each with $2,000 in cash. At the hotel, I tossed the money on my bed along with my meal allowance from the Angels, and it came to about $2,500. So long, Skippy peanut butter! The first thing I did was call room service. It isn't cheap in New York; just a cheeseburger and Coke set me back $25. But I didn't have to worry about that anymore.

It was quite a day. I had fulfilled my childhood dream to play in the big leagues and already had more cash in my hand than I'd ever had in my life.

*   *   *

The next night I got a clean single up the middle off Melido Perez for my first big league hit. As is customary when a rookie gets his first hit, time was called and the ball was tossed into the dugout for me to keep. At first trainer Rick Smith nabbed it, but I knew I was in trouble when I saw Bert Blyleven heading toward Smitty with a sly grin on his face. I knew about Bert's reputation for mischief, and sure enough, when I looked at the ball later he had scrawled on it, "A 60-hopper that barely trickled through the infield." I still laugh every time I see it in my trophy case.

The next day I hit my first major league home run. Facing Scott Sanderson, I hit an inside fastball that hooked around the left-field foul pole. I have that ball, too, thanks to pitcher Mike Butcher, who negotiated a deal with the fan who caught it. I think it cost me a couple of bats. All in all, it was not a bad first weekend in the Bronx. Looking back, I am proud of the fact that it all began in Yankee Stadium. To get your first at-bat, base hit, and home run in the same box where Joe DiMaggio and Mickey Mantle stood is pretty special.

After the Yankees series, we flew on to Baltimore to play the Orioles at Camden Yards. The first game of the series was on August 24, my birthday. I couldn't have asked for a better birthday celebration than to be playing in the big leagues. As is customary for the visiting team, our pregame stretch was in the grass behind the batting cage. The Orioles were in the middle of their batting practice as I took in the beauty of the new Camden Yards. I have to say that there isn't a better seat in the house than right there watching your childhood heroes like Cal Ripken Jr. take batting practice. Fans began to stream down the aisles, signaling that the gates were open. Above our dugout, a throng of fans gathered, hoping to get an autograph when something caught my eye that totally surprised me. A couple of fans were holding up signs that read "Happy Birthday!" A little embarrassed by the attention, I avoided eye contact, fearing they might call out to me. After enduring the abuse of New York's Bleacher Creatures, this was more like it. I could only shake my head in astonishment at the warmth and generosity of the Baltimore fans. What a fantastic welcome for a guy who'd been in the bigs for only a few days. I sat there on the grass taking it all in and kind of digging myself.

Meanwhile, as the Orioles were finishing up batting practice, shortstop Cal Ripken Jr. was the last one out of the cage. All of a sudden the place went nuts. People started waving my birthday signs and singing "Happy Birthday." Not to me, of course—nobody had any idea who I was—but to Ripken, the hometown hero. It turns out that August 24 is his birthday, too. Thank heavens I didn't stand up and tip my cap! I love to share that story with people as a reminder not to let things go to your head. It's natural when you become a big-league ballplayer to think you're something pretty special. That early lesson in humility taught me to keep my ego in check. Later, when I got to know Cal, I told him what happened that day. He loved it. Every time after that, when we played in Baltimore in August, Cal would yell, "Hey, birthday boy! We got a big day this month, don't we?"

It was great to have that special connection with a true legend of the game. There are certain guys after whom you try to model yourself. The way Cal handled himself on and off the field made him the perfect role model; he had such class and dignity. There are a handful of players I played against for whom, because of their involvement in the community and with kids, I have the utmost respect. Cal Ripken Jr. is definitely among them. Sharing these memories of Cal with my grandchildren will be a joy someday.

chapter 4

Building a Foundation

Rookie of the Year, 1993

I played 23 games with the big club in 1992, and though I hit just .177, the Angels saw enough to make me their starting right fielder the following season. During that off-season, I was named Minor League Player of the Year by *Baseball America*. I believe that it had something to do with the Angels' commitment to me going into the winter. That same winter the Angels also made a significant philosophical change to their approach. They decided to go with the young players in the organization who were deserving of a shot. In addition, the club made a trade that shocked most Angels fans. The beloved Jim Abbott was shipped off to the Yankees in exchange for some young talent. J.T. Snow and Russ Springer were the notables in that trade that would round out a core of young, homegrown talent including Chad Curtis, Gary DiSarcina, Damion Easley, John Orton, Mike Butcher, Scott Lewis, Joe Grahe, and me. Today it is nothing to see rosters full of young players, but back then it was a new approach. It usually means one thing: rebuilding.

In 1993 we finished a disappointing fifth in our division. It may have been tough on the fans, but it was a great opportunity for all of us young players to cut our teeth without fear of repercussions. Looking back, I was extremely lucky to be on a club that was rebuilding. Every

Marci has stood by me through the best and the worst. Here we are accepting my Minor League Player of the Year award in 1992. Photo courtesy of the author

day, we were told to just go out there and play, and I ended up hitting .283 with 31 HR and 95 RBIs. My season was cut two weeks short when a sinking line drive off the bat of Larry Sheets jammed my ring finger in my glove and broke it. It came on the heels of my first grand slam, which I had hit just an inning earlier. After the game Buck Rodgers came into the training room to get the news. After hearing the diagnosis that I would need three pins in my finger, he looked at me, raised up his hands, and said, "It never kept me from playing." Every one of his fingers jutted off in every direction but straight. All those years as a catcher had made a mess of his hands. He then let out a grin and congratulated me on a great rookie year.

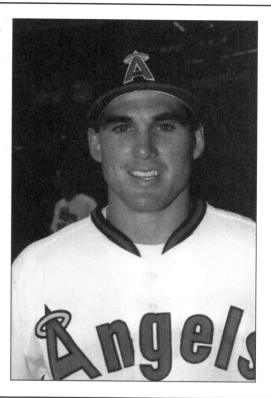

As a fresh-faced rookie in 1992, I hit the ground running and never looked back. Photo courtesy of Joey Cooperman

The patience not to call me up in 1992 had paid big dividends for the organization and me. When I finally got the call in late August, I played in only 23 games in the season, and a wrist injury limited my play enough for me to maintain rookie status for the 1993 season. By the end of my first full season, in 1993, I was named American League Rookie of the Year. Receiving the award and the accolades that went with it strengthened my conviction that I was here to stay. Across town in Los Angeles, another rookie named Mike Piazza claimed the same distinction in the National League. Later that winter the Dodgers did something to recognize his accomplishments and save some money in the long run. They gave Mike a

I have known Mike Piazza since my days in rookie ball. To be named 1993 Rookie of the Year along with him was a great honor.

long-term deal after just one season of play, totally out of the norm for baseball at the time. Of course, the Dodgers would save some money not having to go to arbitration with Mike in a couple of years, but he got the financial security of a big payday. Not to be outdone by the Dodgers, the Angels made a similar offer to me. After an agreement to terms, I suddenly found myself in the most unusual position of not having to worry about my financial future. So much had happened in just a year's time.

I would have never dreamed things would turn out like they did. But the best thing about being Rookie of the Year was the confidence it gave me. I proved it to myself and to everyone else that I belonged in the big leagues. Winning the award and getting the long-term deal proved that I was going to be in the big leagues to stay.

One of the great highlights for me that season was learning to hit under the tutelage of Chili Davis and playing behind all-star pitchers Mark Langston and Chuck Finley. Watching them take the hump was a real treat. Langer and Fin were among the best starters in baseball; we just didn't have the overall depth of talent to win. Offensively, we had a lot of good young hitters, but our inexperience was responsible for much of our stumbles both in 1993 and '94. Veterans like Chili Davis emphasized the team concept, but most of us young guys were focused more on just trying to survive. There were more than a few times at the plate when I was just trying to make contact, never mind figuring out how to get the runner over. In those early years, we were an exciting club, at times full of promise. But it would take a few more years for us to come into our own. It wasn't until 1995 that things finally started to come together. That's when the prophetic voice of Joe Maddon started to ring true.

Chili Dawg

Chili Davis

When I think of the players who have had the most influence on my baseball career, the one who always comes to mind first is Chili Davis. In 1993 we had a lot of inexperienced young players on the Angels. Management looked to Chili to serve as our role model, to show us how to play the game in the big leagues. He was the perfect guy for the situation. He took us all under his wing and gave many of us the foundation for long, productive careers. A lot of guys with his veteran experience and status would not have had the patience to be part of a rebuilding situation. But he took on the challenge and exemplified everything a major leaguer should be. To Chili, going to the ballpark

The help and support Chili Davis gave me in my first few seasons left an indelible mark on my entire career.

wasn't about clocking in and clocking out. He got there early, did the job, and stayed late helping the other guys do their jobs better.

Physically, Chili was one imposing dude. He was incredibly strong, and that bald, bullet head made him look very intimidating. But there was nothing at all ominous about his personality. No one was more approachable. During the season, a ballplayer lives in a clubhouse with 24 other guys, and with so many different things going on at once, the easy thing to do is develop tunnel vision and worry only about yourself. But Chili never did. You could always see him sitting back at his locker holding court with a reporter or younger player or observing the chemistry in the clubhouse. If he saw something going on that needed his attention, he'd be right over to address the situation.

During my first few years with the Angels, Chili hit right behind me in the order. Providing the intimidating protection any young player would dream of, Chili gave me the security of knowing my back was always covered in any hitting situation. Talk about a confidence boost! I wish I had a dollar for all the times he walked up to me as I stood in the on-deck circle eyeing the opposing pitcher and he'd say, "Hey, Fish, how are you going to approach this guy? What's your game plan?" I'd fumble around for an answer, knowing that no matter what I said, he probably had some good advice to add to it. He'd say, "Okay, that's not a bad plan, but what if you tried this?" Chili's experience gave him great insight into what pitchers were thinking, and he helped pass that on to me. As a rookie trying to get established in the lineup, having him looking over my shoulder and whispering in my ear was an unbelievable gift.

It seemed to me at times that Chili could read pitchers' minds. Often I'd be on-deck and he would come up and say, "Fish, this guy's not going to give you anything to hit right here. Try to make him throw you your pitch, but if it's not there don't force it." I listened, and instead of being too aggressive and possibly getting myself out, I would draw a walk, and Chili would do the RBI work behind me. On cross-country flights, Chili always sat in the back of the plane, stretched out across the aisle. A bunch of us young guys sat back there with him, hanging on every word he said. We might talk hitting the whole time or listen to him talk about how he came up with the Giants. The guy was a one-man College of Baseball Knowledge.

As I said before, he was a very imposing figure. He had a black belt in judo, and if you ever saw him break a baseball bat over his knee like it was made out of bamboo, you knew he was not someone you ever wanted to provoke. I'll never forget one incident in Texas that happened early on in my career. A rain delay pushed back the start time. The game finally started, but periodic rain kept further delaying us, taking the game late into the night. League rules said if the game wasn't finished by 1:00 AM, it had to be suspended until the following day. Well, the rain didn't cooperate, so the next day we had to finish it up before starting the game scheduled for that day.

Kevin Brown was scheduled to pitch for Texas, and the Rangers decided he might as well warm up for the assignment by finishing off the previous night's game first. Unfortunately for Brown, we got a couple runs off him in an inning or two to win that game. His frustration became apparent in the second. After a clutch hit drove in couple runs, Brown threw a pitch high and tight to Chili. He would probably deny any intentions, but from our dugout, the pitch had frustration written all over it. Chili was just able to get his head out of the way, but it was clear Brown had just woke a sleeping bear. Chili didn't do anything at the time, but after the game he told me, "Fish, Kevin Brown and I are going to have a little talk tomorrow." From the tone of his voice, I don't think he had exchanging favorite recipes in mind.

During the Rangers' batting practice the next day, Brownie was out in right field shagging fly balls. When it was our turn to bat, I headed to right myself, to shag from my normal position, when a large blur passed me. It was Chili making a beeline to confront Brownie before he jogged off the field. I knew it was going to be interesting, so I picked up my pace, so as not to miss any fireworks. Chili called out to Brownie as he was running off the field.

"Hey, Chili. What's up, dog?" Brown called out casually, as if the figure coming for him was interested in making a social call.

Chili bypassed the pleasantries. "Don't you ever 'Dog' me," he screamed at Brown. "You don't know me that well!"

Now, Kevin Brown was no slouch. He was big and ripped, too, but he knew enough to keep it shut when Chili got right into his face and said, "Look, Brownie! If you ever throw one at my head again, I'm going to come out there and break your friggin' neck! You hear me?"

I stood there watching with my jaw hanging down around my ankles, thinking, *Oh my gosh! Here we go!*

Brownie had enough sense to downplay it through denials and compliments toward Chili. For a moment I wasn't sure it would be enough to mollify him, but it was. Chili backed off ever so slightly and Kevin saw it as his opportunity to resume his jog back to the dugout. No doubt everyone who witnessed it had a newfound respect for Chili. It was impressive. But that was Chili. He was one of the most likable guys around and would do anything he could for you. But when somebody did him wrong or tried to show him up, heaven help that poor soul. Needless to say, Chili never had any more trouble with Kevin Brown—or really anyone I ever saw.

Chili flew very much under the radar except among his peers. He went to Kansas City after he left us, and he had the same effect on a lot of their young guys, too. I've run across a few of them over the years, and everyone says the same thing: Chili Davis brought an intangible to their club that was huge. He was one of those rare individuals who understood and shared the finer points of the game so that everybody got what they needed to be successful. His time mentoring was more than paid back later in his career, when he joined the Yankees and helped them win a few World Series titles.

I have the greatest respect for Chili. He always had time for anybody who wanted to learn and grow as a ballplayer. A team with a young roster needs a guy like that, and with his wealth of knowledge, commanding presence, and love of the game, he ought to be a permanent fixture in the dugout somewhere in the major leagues. There are plenty of young guys in the majors now who would probably sacrifice half their astronomical salaries just to have someone like Chili around to explain things to them. I'm awfully glad to have come up when I did. I don't like to think about what kind of player I would have ended up if Chili hadn't shown me the ropes. Talk to Garret Anderson, Jimmy Edmonds, and some of the other guys, and they'll say the same thing.

Rod Carew

When I look back on my career, I think about how many Hall of Fame players I was lucky to come in contact with. One I appreciate most is my first hitting coach, Rod Carew. A legend in his own right, Rod was able to continue his excellence off the field as he articulated the finer points of hitting to a bunch of rookies in 1993.

Sometimes, because their talent is innate rather than crafted from the toils of extra work and frustration, a lot of superstars don't often appreciate the average guy who struggles just to achieve respectability. Rod Carew was different in this way. I think he always held the belief that anyone could achieve exceptional talent if he understood and worked hard enough at the fundamentals of hitting. As a hitting coach, he always had a great rapport with players, especially those who were willing to be one of his disciples. To me, it showed he cared about us and I really appreciated that quality in him.

During games he'd always have the younger hitters sit next to him in the dugout. Sometimes even the pitchers hung around, trying to glean anything they could off of him. He assigned a chart to one of the bench players to track the types of pitches that were thrown to each of our hitters in games. It proved to be valuable at a time when advance scouting wasn't nearly what it is today. Some of my best growth as a hitter came from his coaching.

There are so many facets to hitting. Some players like the mechanical approach, and some like the mental approach. Going back to my great experience in Triple A, I learned that what works best for me was not focusing so much on the mechanics of what my body was doing but rather my state of mind. The work I did with Rod was never mechanical but analytical. We never broke it down like he might have done with other guys. With me, his focus was primarily on the pitchers, helping me develop a game plan I could take to the plate. Like Chili Davis, Rod really made me understand the concept of pitching strategies, which made me think about what I needed to anticipate standing in the batter's box.

Early in my career, when I didn't always have a game plan, I'd say to Rod, "What's this pitcher trying to do here? What should I be looking for?" He'd say something like, "Fish,

His diligent approach, keen wit, and insights into hitting made hitting coach Rod Carew someone to admire and respect. Photo courtesy of Getty Images

you're gonna see all sliders right here," and he was usually right. His knowledge of the game was tremendous.

He took a team approach to hitting. He frequently held pregame meetings for hitters, and he'd go around the room asking everybody pertinent questions. "Fish, what are you looking for against this guy? What do you know about this rightie coming out of the bullpen?" Or he'd say to GA, "Garret, you've got a lefty coming out of the pen. How has he pitched you in the past? What have you done against him lately?" By drawing out our own knowledge and then adding his own, he really prepared us for the different pitchers we would face from night to night. Just as important, I found out that I could learn something new about a pitcher by hearing my teammates share their keys to hitting a certain guy.

Rod was also one of the game's great pranksters. His favorite targets were rookies, and early in the season he would always make them ride in the bathroom during bus trips. If there was only one rookie it was no big deal, but when we had five or six rooks on the roster, they all had to pile in there, like 1950s college students in a phone booth. Often the ride from the stadium to the airport or to the hotel took around 30 minutes; Rod had them crammed into that tiny john the entire time.

In the mid-'90s we had a rookie pitcher named Mark Holzemer. Mark was a good-natured guy who knew that Rod loved him; he always took his hazing in the fun spirit in which it was intended. But that also made him one of Rod's favorite targets. One night, after a long road trip, we were coming home from Ontario Airport, and Rod gave Holzy his usual marching orders: "Get in the toilet, rook!"

Holzy did as instructed, to everyone else's enjoyment. It was very late, and after the long drive to the stadium, everybody staggered off the bus, went to their cars, and drove home. The bus was heading back to the terminal when the driver almost drove off the road because there was Mark Holzy tapping him on the shoulder and wondering what was going on. He'd fallen asleep in the can, and everybody had forgotten he was in there. The bus driver had to turn around and take Holzy back to the stadium. When everyone found out about it the next day, the story became an instant classic.

As an everyday player, I was usually exempt from Rod's pranks. But Luis Polonia wasn't so lucky. He and Rod used to exchange some real doozies. After Luis found his spikes nailed to the bottom of his locker, for instance, he stole Rod's street clothes from his locker, soaked them in water, and froze them solid before hanging them back up. The game was on! It was fashionable for guys to wear leather pants in the early '90s, and Polonia had a pair that he wore often. One day during the game Rod sneaked up to the clubhouse to do some of his own special tailoring. Taking the pants out of Luis' locker, Rod went to work with some scissors. After the game, when Polonia put on his pants, he discovered that the back pockets were missing, exposing his cheeks, and the legs were cut six inches shorter. Since Luis seldom bothered wearing underwear, it was quite a sight.

Rod's greatest contribution to our team was his emphasis on communication. He was instrumental in reestablishing that old-school part of the game among our group of hitters, and he forged a strong link between the new and old generations that was invaluable. For a Hall of Famer like him to take the time and effort to share his knowledge of the game with anybody who was interested made him as unique as a coach as he was a player.

Nolan Ryan

Breaking into the big leagues as a rookie is the most exciting time of anyone's career. Every day there is something new to experience. Each dawn felt like Christmas morning. Discovering new ballparks and cities always served as a reminder that I had made it to the top, I was a big leaguer. Sometimes when I walked onto a field and saw my childhood heroes out there with me, I felt intimidated. Stepping out under the lights with those superstars made me feel so unworthy at times. Sometimes I would have felt more comfortable admiring them from a distance in the stands like the fans that came to see them. One guy in particular who really gave me that sense of awe was Nolan Ryan. Ryan ranks among the greatest pitchers in baseball history, but

To be able to someday tell my grandkids I hit off Mr. Nolan Ryan is something I hold very dear. Photo courtesy of the Texas Rangers

by the time I had the opportunity to face the legendary hurler, he was at the end of his career. The stuff he was throwing wasn't quite as fearsome as it had been in his prime. Don't get me wrong—his stuff was decent for sure, but it was almost as if I imagined that the pitches coming at me harder then they actually were because of his reputation.

Going up against a Nolan Ryan, you always battled his mystique and aura as much as his pitches. As a kid I heard all the stories about the great Nolan Ryan. I knew he was one of those old-school guys like Carlton Fisk who appreciated players who respected the game. I also knew that he had a penchant for showing up rookies who looked a little too comfortable facing him, brushing them back at the slightest excuse. With that in mind, the first time I stood 60'60" in front of him with a bat in my hand, I wasn't sure if I should swing my bat or just lay it at his feet like a token offering. I remember actually thinking, *Maybe I'll just let him strike me out.* I was truly in awe of his legendary status. It was as if I were a spectator watching my own at-bat. I remember being transfixed as Ryan went into that familiar high leg kick, and the next thing I heard was the sound of his fastball popping into the catcher's mitt and the crowd oohing in admiration of the called strike. *This is for real*, I thought. *He's throwing it to me. I can swing the bat.* Then something even more mind-blowing became apparent. He had thrown a fastball, but it actually hadn't been that fast, maybe 92 miles per hour. Then came the realization, with almost the impact of a Ryan beanball: *I can hit that!*

Once I realized I could actually hit the great Nolan Ryan, I settled down and ended up whacking a big curveball down the left-field line for a double. If Ryan had started yelling at me as I took off down the base path, "Hey, rook! What do you think you're doing?" it's entirely possible that I would've stopped in shock and embarrassment and left it at a single. Thank goodness he ignored me, and I guiltily stretched it into a double. He didn't even try to take my head off in my next at-bat.

That game was the only time I faced him, but I do remember another encounter I had with him after his last start in Anaheim Stadium in 1993. It was before they remodeled the stadium, and it seated something like 60,000 people. I was on the disabled list at the time, so I got to be a fan for the night, but in a better seat—the dugout. The game was sold out, which was rare in Anaheim at the time. The flashbulbs went off with every pitch Ryan threw. I still remember the roar of the crowd as he walked of the field for the last time in Anaheim Stadium. After the game, Chad Curtis, J.T. Snow, and I were working out in our weight room when he walked in. Let me set the scene: in the old stadium, the weight room was basically an oversized storage closet with some machines and weights packed into it. The funky setting meant that you practically climbed over each other to do your different workouts. Because it was the only weight room, the home team had first dibs on it. The visiting team would usually have to wait at least 45 minutes after the game to work out. So you can imagine the surprise we had when about five minutes later Nolan walked in. "You boys mind if I do some exercises?" he said, as if we all belonged on the same planet. When I overcame my astonishment and recovered the power of speech, I managed to whisper, "Do whatever you like, Nolan." My answer would probably have been exactly the same if he had said, "You boys mind if I pick up this dumbbell and crush your skulls with it?" What were we going to say, "No, come back in 45 minutes?" All I could think about was staying out of his way. But he was a true gentleman. Realizing the typical protocol for the situation, he was very appreciative that we let him get his workout done early.

Nolan Ryan retired from baseball that same year. Having a chance to bat against him and managing a hit off him is something I'll enjoy telling my grandchildren about. And spending a half-hour or so pumping iron with him is a memory I will always treasure.

The Big Three
Mark Langston, Jim Abbott, and Chuck Finley

Looking back at the teams we fielded in the 1990s, it amazes me that we didn't win more than we did. Our Big Three—Mark Langston, Chuck Finley, and Jim Abbott—were among the best pitchers on the mound in that era. And our bullpen wasn't too shabby, either. If it wasn't Troy Percival closing out for us, it was Lee Smith or Bryan Harvey.

Offensively speaking, we had a lot of young hitters during those years, and we could do some great things at times. But our inexperience probably led to a few more letdowns than an experienced club would have had. Looking back at the offensive juggernauts in Cleveland, New York, Baltimore, Texas, and even Seattle, you could see the difference. We could put up 10 runs in a heartbeat against average pitching, but facing a No. 1 or 2 starter when it counted was a little out of our reach.

(From left) Jim Abbott, Chuck Finley, and Mark Langston absolutely dominated the opposition during my tenure with the Angels.

The Big Three went out there every night and kept us in the game, but somehow we still couldn't win consistently. The Angels' pitching staffs over the past few years have been very good but I don't necessarily see them as better than what we had back then. So why, then, do the Angels teams of today win more than we did back then? Depth! Our problem back then was that even though we had great arms in the first three slots, we lacked the complementary pieces of the puzzle. We had three real aces and a good closer, but our fourth and fifth starters always seemed to be question marks. This was true every spring. To win, we needed the kind of depth the Angels have today. Look at any team that wins nowadays and you will always see depth in its starting rotation.

As a young player, I was in awe of some of the performances I saw on the hill from night to night. When Mark Langston took the hump in his prime, he was as filthy as they came. A natural athlete, Langer could have played anywhere on the ballfield and excelled. In fact, he was so multitalented he could have been a professional soccer player, musician, or who knows, maybe even a brain surgeon. It would have been fascinating to tap into that mind and find out what made him tick. Gifted with a devastating curveball, hitters seemed to always come up with mysterious ailments when he pitched. It was amazing to see the most seasoned hitters around the league reduced to knee-buckling average Joes when they faced him.

He was a real treat to play behind, as well, because you always knew we had a great shot at coming out on top. Games were relatively short as hitters looked to put the first fastball in play, avoiding that nasty curve at all costs. One game always stands out in my mind. It was against Baltimore sometime in the mid-'90s, when they had all the bashers. Langer cruised into the eighth inning maybe giving up one or two hits. The game wasn't even two hours old and I had barely broken a sweat on defense. He had reduced that explosive offense into a bunch of Little Leaguers. I mean no disrespect. I count it a blessing to have never faced him.

My favorite memory of Langer took place off the field, when he introduced me to my favorite band of all time, Rush. An avid musician and guitar player, Langer developed a relationship over the years with Geddy Lee, the lead singer from the band. One year, playing in Toronto, Geddy came out to the ballpark to hang with the team. I was in heaven. It got even better the next day when we were invited to their studio to see the work they were doing on a new album. It was amazing to be around such rock legends, and they were big baseball fans as well. Geddy asked a lot of questions about the game, and we asked him about the music industry. I came away from that experienced convinced that all musicians would love to be professional athletes and all athletes would love to be rock stars. It must be the limelight.

One of my all-time favorite players to be around was Chuck Finley. Fin was a fun-loving guy who had a self-depreciating sense of humor. To hear him talk at times you'd think he was just an average pitcher; in reality, though, he was one of the best in the game. I remember the first time I met him, in my first big-league camp. He treated me with a respect you wouldn't expect from a veteran of his caliber. A really funny guy to be around, Fin was always cracking a joke or saying something witty. Bus rides to and from the airport were always filled with laughter coming from his seat in the back of the bus. He was the veteran guy in the back of the plane telling jokes or sitting at the poker table holding down the best seat in the house.

Fin could always lighten the mood when needed or bring it seriousness. He was an unquestioned leader in the clubhouse and he had the respect of all the players and staff. There was no guessing where you stood with Fin. He wore his emotions on his sleeve and always told it to you straight. I'll never forget the time when we were going through a tough slide, and GM Billy Bavasi and a few of the coaches came into the locker room to light a fire under us. They yelled and carried on, figuring it would goad us out of our funk, but instead it just got everybody upset. Finally, an emotional Fin stood up, looked around, and said, "I know there's not one of you in here that's giving up. Every one of you guys I'd go into battle for." And that's all it took. Just about every man in that locker room was thinking the same as I was. With just those two sentences, Fin had us ready to walk through fire. Having leadership like that is irreplaceable.

His feats on the field were just as awesome. Whenever the benches cleared for a brawl, it was Fin who made it his mission to take out the biggest guy on the other team. Fin might have looked like a beanpole, but when you saw him in the weight room, you realized how tough he was. During one brawl with the Oakland A's, he yanked Mark McGwire from the pile and whisked him off the field. Big Mac was in a rage, screaming, "You're crazy, man! You're crazy!" But Fin, employing a stiff-arm that would have made any NFL running back envious, just kept moving McGwire away from the fight. He did the same thing to Mo Vaughn once. Fin just grabbed him and walked him right out of the pile. It was the most amazing thing I ever saw. Mac and Mo didn't want to fight Fin, not so much because they were afraid of him, but because they respected him. He was one strong dude, but his real strength was in the way he carried himself.

Of all the guys I played with, Jim Abbott was probably the one I related to best. Abbie was a humble competitor and a real fan favorite. I always remember him signing autographs for anyone who approached him. A genuinely nice guy, it seemed he just couldn't say no to a kid. It always struck me that if a superstar like him couldn't turn away a fan, how could I? One thing the fans probably never saw was his incredible desire to perform well. His competitive nature might surprise anyone who ever saw him in the dugout. When things didn't go his way, he went downstairs to really let loose, out of the view of the fans. He didn't show a lot of emotion in public, but behind the scenes he could be volcanic. Some of my own teammates might say the same about me. As much as I wanted to control my emotions, sometimes you just have to let it blow!

Jim had an above-average fastball, but his most lethal weapon was a cutter that broke inside on right-handed batters. I have never seen more broken bats than on days he pitched. It got so that teams started making extreme adjustments, such as hitting lefties instead of righties in an effort to change it up on him. Much like Mariano Rivera today, a pile of broken bats were left in his wake whenever Abbie pitched. During his second stint with us, Abbie lost some of his velocity and tried to compensate by mixing in different pitches. Unfortunately, things didn't go as well for him and he faded from the game like most of us do when we lose whatever it was that got us there. But as far as I'm concerned, no one had more guts and fighting spirit than Abbie.

chapter 5

Friends and Adversaries

Opposites Attract

Chad Curtis

Chad Curtis was one of the most confident players I have ever been around. Growing up, he was the smallest kid on the block and he always had to fight harder than anyone else to get to where he wanted to be. Always considered the long shot, he developed a chip on his shoulder that turned out to be his greatest asset. He brought that same fiery temperament with him to the big leagues.

My relationship with Chad began in my junior year at Grand Canyon College. I was highly touted going into my draft year, which meant there would be a lot of scouts coming to our games. Chad transferred into GCC knowing that it would be a great opportunity for exposure. We became pretty good friends that year and have been ever since.

Not many people could overcome the odds stacked against him, but he figured it out. But along the way he got labeled as being too stubborn. To understand Chad, you have to know that everything is a personal challenge to him. If you don't agree with something he believes, he will take it on as a challenge to bring you around to his

My best friend and college roommate, Chad Curtis. Photo courtesy of the author

way of thinking. He is a very intelligent person, so most of his arguments are well supported. That is his personality: he's always primed for a good argument or challenge.

Such was the case when he came to GCC. His goal was to get drafted and someday play in the big leagues. In his very calculated way of thinking, he came to GCC to play alongside me to show the scouts that he was just as deserving of their consideration. In his mind, there was never a doubt he could outplay me, and in truth, he probably did that year. When draft time came around, we both ended up drafted by the Angels, but at two different spectrums. I went in the third round and he went in the 45th.

This was a typical example of the odds that Chad always had stacked against him. For him, being drafted high was just another log on the fire that stoked his passion and a chance to prove the world wrong. He couldn't wait to sign a contract, get on the field, and show the Angels' scouts how wrong they were to take him so late. His greatest dream was to play in the big leagues, and he wasn't going to waste any time getting there. He wanted nothing more than to show everybody that he belonged on a big-league ballfield *today*.

We both signed with the Angels and ended up going to short season and Instructional League together. Rooming with him, I saw just how fanatical he was about chasing his dream. As a kid, he had his life all mapped out. "I'm going to play in the big leagues," he used to tell me. "Then someday I'm going to break all of Pete Rose's records." It was pretty heady stuff for someone who hadn't made it past Instructional League. Personally, I couldn't see myself getting out of Class A ball, let alone playing in the big leagues.

The Angels had Chad playing different positions than he was accustomed to playing. Pegged as an infielder because of his size, he had an unbelievable challenge ahead of him trying to learn a new position. In the beginning it almost hurt to watch. He looked like a fish out of water. They were basically telling him, "Sink or swim, kid. Figure it out for yourself."

As Chad's friend, I hated to see it. But I also knew that everything that happened motivated him further. I'm convinced that if things had gone any easier for him, he wouldn't have succeeded. He is the type of guy who actually needs someone in his face screaming, "You can't do it!" For as long as I've known him, there has always been someone or something there telling him he can't do it—and he has made it his life's goal to prove them wrong. His ability to adapt and overcome is one of the reasons Chad rose through the ranks faster then I did. While I was in Double A learning how to hit, he was at Triple A getting primed for the majors. Then he caught his big break: an opportunity to play winter ball in

Venezuela. Then everything everything around for him after he won the batting title. Next stop: the bigs.

I was in Triple A the year Chad made the Angels' big club. He ended up being my biggest booster and PR guy, telling anybody who would listen, "Hey, my buddy Timmy, he's doing real well in Edmonton. You need to take a good look at him." It was nice to have somebody banging the drum for me like that.

When I got the call-up later that summer, the Angels were on the road playing in New York. Chad came bounding into the clubhouse during batting practice and greeted me like a long-lost brother. We were best friends, and it was quite a moment of celebration being in Yankee Stadium together. The end of that year saw some other young prospects get called up and Chad gave them the red-carpet treatment as well. He took a lot of us under his wing, and I can't think of anybody who didn't benefit from it.

Chad has a great heart, but he could also rub some people the wrong way. He was never afraid to say what he thought, and he wasn't always diplomatic about it. Not everyone appreciated his frank personality. In 1994 he and Rod Carew, the Angels' hitting coach at the time, butted heads over hitting philosophies. Coincidence or not, he was dealt to Detroit for Tony Phillips shortly thereafter.

Sent packing, Chad was understandably disappointed, but going to Detroit meant that he would get to play back home in Michigan. A change of scenery did him good for a while, and his game settled in. Chad established himself as a scrappy player with some wheels, and he got the attention of playoff teams looking to add some speed to their club as the trade deadline approached. Always known as a tough competitor, Chad established himself as a hired gun for teams in the postseason mix. Stints in Los Angeles and Cleveland eventually got him the exposure that brought the Yankees calling.

Chad ended up playing a key role for the Yankees during their championship run in the late '90s. He had some big hits for them, including one game-winning walk-off homer in the World Series. When he retired in 2001, he left the game with a couple championship rings, but Pete Rose's records were still intact. Interestingly, by the end of his career, instead of being the aggressive and free-swinging hitter I knew, Chad finally learned to be patient, taking pitches and drawing walks. He was smart enough to realize that getting on base and working the count were qualities that teams looked for in older player. Eventually he showed that he was capable of listening to others' advice. Maybe he wasn't as stubborn as some people thought.

People who know both Chad and me always say, "You guys were best friends? No way!" We seem like such polar opposites that most people can't believe we got along so well. Sure, sometimes he would say things I could never have dreamed of saying, but it never affected our friendship one bit. We are living proof, I guess, that opposites do attract.

"Ratboy"

Gary DiSarcina

One of the toughest things about winning in World Series in 2002 was not being able to celebrate on the field with a player who had a tremendous influence on many of our lives. Gary DiSarcina was the heartbeat of the Angels teams in my early years. A natural leader, everyone looked to him for insight and direction, and when things needed firing up. Every team needs a guy who stirs things up once in a while and holds everyone accountable for their jobs. "Disar" was a throwback of sorts who insisted that you appreciate the game by playing it the right way, not by showing people up. If you stepped out of that mold around him, watch out. "Ratboy" would call you on it.

Tenacious, intense, and driven, Gary DiSarcina was a true leader and friend.

I think that Gary Gaetti was the original Ratboy, but because he and Disar were lockermates, it was passed down when Gaetti was released. The name fit Disar as well or better because he was skinny and wiry and had a bit of a schnoz that resembled a rat's. His surly, prickly disposition had something to do with it, too. He always seemed to be agitated, as if he had a burr in his underwear or something. I think part of that was his unquenchable desire to win—and in those days, nothing came easy for us. Sure, we won our fair share of games, but it was due more to our grit than an overabundance of talent. I can always remember him talking about how much of a grind the game was. Being a shortstop, where you need laser focus on every play, is more demanding, I'm sure, than playing the outfield. He demanded that the rest of us play the game to his standards. If you didn't, he'd get right in your grill, which he did to me a few times.

Nobody was off limits from Disar's wrath, not even Roger Clemens. In fact, I think he despised guys like the Rocket all the more. Anyone who was on top of his game, making it look easy and having fun with it, really seemed to irk Disar. One night, playing Boston, Rocket was on the mound and dealing. Disar must have picked up on a disrespectful arrogance in the Rocket's game that night. After striking out once, Disar walked all the way back to the dugout staring down Clemens muttering, "I'm gonna get you, you SOB! I'm gonna get you!" When he got to the bench he became a little more vocal about it, drawing a few looks from the mound. Sitting on the bench taking this in, I thought, *Based on the swings you just took, Disar, I don't think you have any chance getting him tonight, but I certainly applaud your confidence.* But that was Disar, and his attitude rubbed off on all of us. His credo was: Make it personal and never give up. Anytime he was beat, he always came clawing back, got in your face, and challenged you.

This attitude prevailed off the field as well. If something wasn't right in the clubhouse or away from the field and needed to be addressed, he'd do it. Seeing the situation exactly how it was, he cut through all the bull and got right to the point. At team meetings he never yelled—but he didn't have to. You always knew that when he was talking, you'd better listen. But he would fight for you just as easily as he'd rip you a new one. If the opposing pitcher threw high and tight at one of our guys, Gary would be the one on the top step of the dugout screaming and calling the pitcher every name in the book. He would also be the one to hang around the clubhouse after the game and offer encouragement to those who needed it.

In 2002 we had a team full of grinders, guys who played every inning hard and never quit. The core of that team set the tone, and all of them benefited from Disar's influence. He was the ultimate team player and a great friend. Not having him with us at the bottom of our World Series celebration pile was a sad omission. But if you asked Percy, Ersty, Orlando, GA, AK, Speez, or me, we'd all tell you that the Ratboy was certainly with us in spirit.

"Timmy Land"

I have been teased throughout my entire life about my naïveté. Maybe it is a product of my upbringing, moving around a lot as a child, but the place where I often find myself is inside my own head. A perfectionist by nature, I created a sort of insulation from the rest of the world. Don't get me wrong, it's not all bad. This ability to block out the world is one of the reasons I've been able to achieve the level of success it took for me to become a big leaguer. In the mid-1990s, Gary DiSarcina coined the phrase "Timmy Land" to describe my state of mind around the clubhouse.

I make it sound like a virtue, but my wife and some teammates would say otherwise. Sometimes when I go into that state of intense focus and isolation, the people around me might as well be talking to a mannequin for all the notice I give to them. I don't mean to be rude; I just have the tendency to be one-track-minded at times. When I'm not in Timmy Land, I think I'm as nice and considerate as anybody. But when my mind is focused on one thing, anybody who wants to tell me about something funny he saw on TV last night would be better off going to the next locker over.

When they got used to it, my teammates actually had a lot fun with Timmy Land. I've been known to make a goofy remark or two. It has provided them endless fodder for jokes and teasing. Rick Smith, the longtime Angels trainer, says that if he had written down all the strange stuff he has heard me say when I was in Timmy Land, he'd have a warehouse full of notebooks. Smitty claims, among other things, that I once complained to him that the ice in the trainer's room was too cold, that I frequently asked, "What time does the 10:00 bus leave?" And that he once heard me order a cheeseburger and tell the waitress, "No cheese." Of course, I would argue the stories get a little better every time they're repeated, but I have to admit my mouth has a tendency to spit out my first thought at times.

Usually I find myself following up most of the things I say with an explanation. For example, Smitty loves to tell one story that three months into the season I had asked, "Who's that Japanese guy in our bullpen?" It was Shigetoshi Hasegawa, who at this point had been with the club about two and a half years.

I caught a lot of grief for it, but I defend myself this way: Shige must have been spot-starting or in the rotation for a short period of time prior to this game. Not aware that he was put back into the bullpen, I might have been caught off guard to see him warming up out there. Making a typical comment to another player like, "Who do we have warming up down there?" could be perceived, based on my history, as, "I don't recognize that pitcher in the 'pen. Is he new?" Anybody else and the response is "Shige!" But, to me, the response is sometimes delayed as they try to get a read on me. It's all good with me, if it makes others smile.

"Wonder Dog"

Rex Hudler

Everybody's heard the cliché, "the thrill of victory and the agony of defeat." For the more squeamish in our clubhouse it was the other way around, as most the time a win for us put the "Wonder Dog" into action. It was quite a show. After one game, Rex Hudler celebrated the W by running the length of the locker room, executing a perfect swan dive across the dining table, then doing a handstand

When they made Rex Hudler, they broke the mold. His hustle and positive outlook inspired everyone.

against the wall and five upside-down pushups. Oh, and the Wonder Dog was wearing only his spikes and hat. If you were there, the spectacle is burned into your brain forever. Perhaps you might question if his act is for real. I can say that in our three years together, I am qualified to say yes. There was nothing phony about him. He was ADHD before it was a thing. People were exhausted just watching him. Then again, I really don't have to convince people of this anymore; most Angels fans can relate having heard him in the broadcast booth.

I first saw him in spring 1994. He was with the San Francisco Giants trying to make their team. In a game at Tempe Diablo Stadium, four unimpressive at-bats totally had my attention. It wasn't his hitting but his amazing hustle. He ran down the first-base line with a zeal I wasn't accustomed to seeing, especially from a freckled redhead. After running out the ball, he'd make his right turn and jog passed our dugout screaming, "Ooooh, did you see that?" I'm not exactly sure what or who he was referring to. I was impressed with how much effort he put into everything. I recall Langer—Mark Langston—telling me at the time, "Fish, we've got to get this guy!" A bum hamstring, I think, didn't help his chances in San Francisco, so the Angels were able to pick him up. After we met him and got our first-hand exposure to his boundless energy, the consensus was, *Okay, there's no way this guy is for real! He can't be like this all the time, can he?*

As I got to see Hud in action, what impressed me the most about him was how he could go a whole week without playing in a game, and then when he finally got into one, he shined like an everyday player. Of course it was all pure adrenaline. I always thought to myself, *Dude, you'll never survive every day playing like that.* But he did. He realized that to survive he had to be a maximum-effort guy, so he always played with the pedal to the metal. As long as he wasn't overexposed, he was a great asset to the team.

He's a character, for sure. A high school football star, he turned down a full-ride football scholarship with the Fighting Irish of Notre Dame. No doubt this boundless energy displayed on game days had its roots in the gridiron. Mr. Steinbrenner of the New York Yankees loved his personality and athleticism enough to do whatever it took to sign him. In the games that found Hud's name in the starting lineup, you had better be on guard because he had all the intensity of an NFL linebacker like Ray Lewis. More than a few times I was brought out of my comfort zone of being cool and collective by a Hud encounter. The most notorious example of this is my now infamous "upstream" handshake. For years it seemed Hud wanted me to give him the upstream whenever I hit a home run or did something significant. I was never too comfortable with this outward display of emotion, but nonetheless it was hard to turn him away when he got all worked up. Waiting at home plate for me after a homerun, Hud would be egging me on to do our upstream handshake as I touched the plate. I was always too embarrassed to give him much of an effort.

That is what was great about Hud. It was never about himself but more about lifting someone else up for his performance. He recognized he would play only once every few days, but rather than complain about it, he embraced the great opportunity he had on those select days. And for such a great competitor, he was also very humble. He always described himself as "just a bootleg player stealing a paycheck." In my opinion he was downgrading himself, but Hud was always very aware of what he did and didn't have. He realized his limitations, but he never dwelled on his shortcomings too much. He embraced his role as a veteran bench player and always made the most of every opportunity.

Back in his playing days, if you threw Hud the ball right down the middle of the plate, he'd swing and miss; but if you threw one in the dirt or over his head, he'd dig it out or tomahawk it for a hit. Just like Vladimir Guerrero today, Hud was such a good bad ball hitter that it was positively scary. Through the years nothing has changed about Hud. He's a character, gifted with uniqueness all his own. I celebrate my friendship with the Wonder Dog—but with my clothes on and my feet firmly planted on the ground.

"Bodacious"

Bo Jackson

My first memory of Bo Jackson goes back to my college days, when I played in the Cape Cod League one summer. On one off-day some teammates and I went to Boston for a Red Sox doubleheader against the Kansas City Royals. We sat behind home plate and watched Bo strike out three consecutive times against Roger Clemens. They had to be the most impressive strikeouts I've ever seen. It was power against power, and Bo was swinging so stinking hard that if he had actually hit the ball, it probably would have landed in Canada.

When Bo joined the Angels in '94, he was already legendary in the world of sports. A promising NFL career cut short due to a hip injury, Bo was reduced to playing just his "hobby" sport, baseball. It was almost too cool to hang with him. He was the Michael Jordan of baseball. It was like hanging out with a rock star.

As a fellow outfielder, I got to spend a lot of time with him that spring. Something I noticed about him was that he never wore metal spikes. Because of a hip injury, he wore the old-style plastic cleats, which were impossible to get from Nike—that is, unless you were Bo Jackson. I told him how I had been trying to get a pair from Nike without much luck. "It sure would be nice to have a pair of those plastic spikes to wear during practice, to save my feet for the game," I told him. I had a bad foot that spring, and it really hurt to wear those metal spikes. "No problem," Bo replied. "Go get yourself a pair out of my locker." He had a ton of plastic spikes stacked on top of his locker. I ran inside and took out a pair only to find they were a size too big. *Oh well, at least they will get me out of my spikes.*

Physically, there was no more impressive a specimen than Bo. He had muscles on top of muscles, and was the kind of guy who could run through a brick wall. When I put his shoes on, I felt I could do the same thing, like the kid Calvin Cambridge in the movie *Like Mike*. I was like a kid again. *These are Bo Jackson's shoes*, I said to myself. *I'm Bo Jackson!*

My favorite memory of Bo stands out vividly, as if it happened yesterday. Every spring, the trainers implemented a weightlifting program for every player to follow after practice. One day, after a hard workout on the field, we were in the weight room when Bo came strolling through on his way out. He was in blue jeans, a tank top, flip-flops, and sunglasses. Tom Wilson, our strength coach yelled at Bo, "Hey, where you going? You too good to lift weights?"

Pausing for a moment by the door, Bo spun around and marched over to the bench press. Declaring in his booming Southern accent, he said, "Bo don't need to lift." Like we needed to be told that. He plopped down on the bench to give us a demonstration you could never forget. The press was set up for us average Joe baseball players, with a 45-pound plate on each side. Bo looked at it for a moment and barked to Tom, "What do you have on that? Throw on some more and get out of the way, boy."

Tom threw on another two plates, bringing the weight close to 300 pounds, and stepped aside. By then everyone in the room had totally stopped what they were doing, waiting to see what was going to happen next. Bo stretched out on the bench and threw up that weight like it was nothing. He did 15 reps so fast I could hardly count them. Then slammed the bar back on the rack, said, "I told you, Bo don't need to lift," got up, and walked out the door! Nobody could believe it. We were all thinking the same thing: *No wonder he ran over linebackers in the NFL.* To see this monster of a man throw that kind of weight around was just amazing.

One of Bo's biggest claims to fame was his speed. He could get down the first-base line faster than anyone in the game, including Willie Wilson, who was considered by many to be the fastest guy in baseball. When Bo hit a two-hopper to the shortstop, you can bet that if it wasn't played just perfectly, it was an infield hit for him. But there was far more to Bo than just brute strength and speed. He was a very classy guy. During plane rides I'd sit with him and listen to him tell stories about his upbringing, growing without a father. Hearing about what he went through and then seeing the kind of a father Bo was to his own kids made me respect him greatly. He was an upfront guy who took the responsibilities of being a father and a role model seriously. He also had a speech impediment that caused him to stutter; seeing him work through that was equally impressive.

The season I played with Bo in 1994 was the strike year. Our last game was against the Royals at home, and everybody knew there was a good chance we might not be back for a while. I think Bo realized it might be his last game ever, so he went all out. After getting on base in his last at-bat, Bo was poised to do what he hadn't done since he'd had his hip replaced. On consecutive pitches, he stole second and then third. He was showing everyone, *I'm going to give everything I've got one more time and play like I used to.* I was totally blown away.

I had so much respect for Bo as an athlete and a friend. He was someone very special in the physical sense, but what impressed me most was the way he treated people. Always kind and considerate, especially for a superstar, Bo always made people feel special. In my book, that's bigger then any touchdown, homer, or stolen base.

G.A.

Garret Anderson

My first memory of Garret Anderson is of him driving into the parking lot at Gene Autry Park in Mesa, Arizona, in a snazzy white Mustang. Seeing a tall, skinny, young kid get out of that eye-popping car, my first thought was, *Whoever he is, I guess we've got to pay attention to him.* A week later, we'd heard a grand total of two words out of him, and I remember thinking then that something didn't match up. I had expected a little more flash and a lot more mouth from a guy who had wheels like that.

He's still the same old G.A. today: calm, cool, and collected. He still likes nice cars, and he still talks as little as possible. I often think that because of his laid-back demeanor and approach, he's been misunderstood throughout much of his career. He is a deep thinker and very aware of the varied perceptions people have of him, but he'll never go out of his way to change for somebody else's sake. Many of us try to conform in situations and please the people around us, but not Garret. He always stays true to himself, no matter what the situation. Throughout his career, people have tried to read into his body language, but the one message Garrett has continuously sent out is: *Hey, I'm comfortable in my skin, I like the way I am, and if you don't like it, that doesn't bother me.*

I've always believed that if you put Garret in a Los Angeles Lakers uniform, people would be talking about him the way they talk about James Worthy. You'd use all the superlatives people use in that game to describe somebody who's smooth on the court. But in baseball, for some reason, it doesn't fly—especially with him. Baseball demands hardnose play with lots of hustle—and getting dirty doing it—but that's just not his style.

An interesting thing happened to me one year in spring training. I had a conversation with our then-manager Terry Collins and outfield instructor Sam Suplizio. They asked for my opinion. "We

My great friend and competitor, the quiet and reserved Garret Anderson.

have a lot of outfielders here, and we're thinking about making a deal to trade one of them. Who would you trade?" At the time, Garret had spent only about a half a season in the big leagues. They had not been around him enough to really know what kind of player he would end up being. Because I had known him the longest they felt it was worth getting my opinion. At the time, we also had a young phenom in Ersty, Jimmy Edmonds and his amazing theatrics in center field, and me. My answer was, "You know, that's not an easy decision. But I will say this: get rid of me before you get rid of Garret Anderson." I knew that he was potentially the real deal, someone who could be counted on every day. There was no doubt in my mind that he was going to hit. To those within the organization it wasn't exactly earth-shattering news, but to those who were new on the scene they needed a little convincing. G.A. is as natural a hitter you'll ever find, and one who will never be intimidated in any situation you put him in.

To really understand Garret, you had to be in his inner circle of friends. His quiet demeanor opens up to a fun-loving personality to those that really know him. He is very much a family man who holds himself to a high moral standard. A man of faith, he could always be counted on to attend chapel and Bible studies on the road with me. When other guys were closing down nightclubs, G.A. could always be found back at the hotel playing cards with a group of like-minded teammates. On the road he was always someone I could count on for lunch or dinner.

I've known G.A. a long time, and he's as good a friend as I've ever had in baseball. But to this day I will call him up and the conversation will go something like this:

"Hey, Garret, what's up?"

"Nothing."

"What are you doing?"

"Nothing."

"Do you want to go out for dinner?

"Sure."

"Where do you want go?

"Wherever"

"What time?"

"Whenever."

"Okaaay!!"

That's just his personality, he doesn't say much, and he really doesn't get excited about anything.

Unfortunately, the same understated but confident personality that friends and baseball people love about him hasn't gone over well with fans. There are those who would prefer their ballplayers to be more demonstrative and emotional on the field. He doesn't give you the smiles and high-fives, and that disappoints some fans. When most players fail, they tend to show some emotion, but Garret shows nothing. I always saw it as one of his strengths, his ability to stay on an even keel. To the average fan, seeing a display of emotion evokes a passion for the game. And when Garret stays the same on the surface, some read that he could care less about what people think; fans can't relate to that. They're out there chewing their knuckles in every situation. When their guy doesn't come through, they lose it, and they want to see their guy get upset, too. So when he just walks back to the dugout as if it was no big deal, they wonder, *Does he even care?*

I suspect, to some extent, that some of his teammates have even asked the same question about him. Those who really get to know him quickly realize that he *does* care. He just has a way of moving right ahead to the next at-bat, while a guy like me might hang on to the one before, analyzing, regretting, and replaying it. Then my next time up, I might make another out because I'm still thinking of the one before. Garret doesn't do that, and that's something the fans can't appreciate about him.

Nobody has changed Garret Anderson. He's his own man and has no trouble living that way. You have to admire a guy like that. It does seem to me that as he's gotten older, he has opened up a little more. What you see in him today is a lot different than what we saw early on in his career. But he remains as solid as they come, a good Christian and family man, and one of the guys I'd always look to hang out with on the road. He is also the best protection a hitter ever could want hitting behind him. So it was fitting and kind of prophetic for me to see him drive in the winning runs that gave the Angels their first world championship.

Lee Smith

In the big leagues, sooner or later everybody develops his own program, his own style of carrying himself and interacting with his teammates. Whether or not that program is accepted depends on his stature in the game. Barry Bonds, I've heard, had his own program, and his teammates accepted it because of what he does on the field. A rookie's program is one story. But when it's a veteran and potential Hall of Famer, you're generally cool with the way he operates because he's earned it.

Lee Smith definitely had his own program. As teammates, I probably didn't get to know him as well as some of the pitchers in the bullpen, but the few times I was around him he was always fun. One of the true heroes of the game, I grew up watching him close out Cubs victories on many summer days in high school. Back in the day before ESPN, you could always count on a Cubs' game on WGN. He just looked huge on TV, dominating so many great hitters of that era.

As a young major leaguer, I was thrilled to have an opportunity late in his career to be his teammate. Meeting him for the first time, I was struck by two things. First, by how enormous his hands were (a baseball looked like a golf ball in his giant hands) and second, by his laid-back personality. He exuded the kind of jolly old Southern attitude you might see from someone sitting on a porch of an old country farmhouse with a straw hat on. He acted as if he didn't have a care in the world. He was a funny guy who made light of things going on around him.

Since I was a position player, I missed out on a lot of the bonding that went on with the pitchers. I got to know Lee more through stories Troy Percival, his fellow pitcher, told me about him. Troy often talked about how Smitty would take naps in the back room of the clubhouse during games. That explained why I never remembered seeing him after the games started. Usually the bullpen would hang around the clubhouse or training room getting warmed up for the first few innings of a game. In the eighth inning, Smitty would come lumbering into the clubhouse from some back room to check in on the score and see if his services would be needed for the night. If not, he'd lumber on back to finish up his snooze. On nights when he was called into the game, it didn't take Smitty long to get warmed up. As a matter of fact, I really believe his slow walk into the game from the bullpen was part of his warmup. Foghat must have been watching Smitty pitch one night when they wrote the song *Slow Ride*, because it fit him to a T.

I always had the utmost respect and counted it a thrill to play with him. A long-standing veteran, Smitty developed his own program, and as one of the game's all-time great relievers, he deserved it. When he played with us he had more saves than anyone in baseball history (478) and guys respected that. He saved 37 games for us in '95 and was a role model for Troy Percival. I'm sure Percy would say that Smitty had a great influence on his own game, so he obviously couldn't have been snoozing *all* the time.

Cal's Big Night

One of my greatest career highlights came on September 6, 1995, when Cal Ripken Jr. broke Lou Gehrig's record for consecutive games played. Everything surrounding that event was surreal, including the Secret Service snipers on the stadium roof because President Bill Clinton and Vice President Al Gore were in attendance. The whole stadium was buzzing, and everybody there, players and fans alike, knew it was a historic event that would be talked about for years to come.

Even under normal circumstances, Camden Yards is a fantastic place to play. The smoke drifting onto the field from Boog Powell's BBQ creates an aura so mystical that you half-expect to look up and see Roy Hobbs striding up to the plate as in *The Natural*. There's always an electric atmosphere in that great ballpark, and this time, of course, it was totally off the grid.

The game became official after we hit in the top of the fifth inning, and when the Orioles came up to bat in their half of the inning, a big banner suddenly unfurled on the warehouse beyond right field, emblazoned with the magic number: 2,131. Ripken had batted in the inning before and had hit a home run—it was one of the most amazing things I had ever seen. I guess breaking the record for most consecutive games wasn't enough.

As Ripken ran around the bases, flashbulbs went off all over the stadium, probably driving those rooftop snipers crazy. Everybody was on their feet cheering for what seemed like a half-hour straight. Of course, I was standing there taking it all in, thinking, *I have the best seat in the house!* After his teammates congratulated him, he retreated into the dugout. They stopped the game and tried to get him to come back out and acknowledge the occasion. Eventually a couple teammates shoved him back onto the field, and he took a victory lap around the field. Watching him run around the track, to what must have been the longest standing ovation ever, gave me goose bumps. The rest of my teammates stood in awe as well. It was just an amazing moment.

I didn't do so badly at the plate myself that night, going 3-for-4 with a homer and a double. They didn't stop the game for me, of course, but my double forced a pitching change. During the lull, I was standing at second base when Cal walked up to me. It was the greatest night of his professional life, and he asked me how my big day was last week. Of course, I knew he meant my birthday, the one we both share on August 24th. I was making small talk with baseball's new Iron Man! "How do you hit a home run like that at just the right moment when everyone is cheering for you? That's amazing. How did you do that?" I asked. He just smiled and shrugged.

We chatted throughout the whole pitching change. Mostly we talked about how special that night was. It was like having a private audience with the Pope. I remember thinking, *I'm in the most enviable position of any person in the stadium.* Of course photographers were taking pictures of him throughout the game, and there were some great shots of us talking. Later a photographer gave me a print of one, and Cal signed it for me.

Earlier in the game I had a big scare. After breaking for second on a missed hit-and-run, my spike got caught up in the webbing of Ripken's glove, and as soon as I hit him I thought, *Oh God, please don't let me be responsible for putting him on the DL. Not tonight!* Fortunately, nothing happened. If something had, I don't think all those snipers plus the entire U.S. Army could have saved me from the angry fans.

Outside of winning the World Series, playing in that game was the biggest honor of my career. What an amazing night. Seeing Cal break the record and on cue hit a home run seemed like something straight out of a Hollywood movie. It just about defied reality.

Every ball used in the game that night had the Cal Ripken logo on it, and because they were historic, every inning we all wanted to be the one to catch the last out and keep the ball. After about the fifth inning I'm thinking, "Man, I've got to get one tonight!" I ended up catching two last-inning outs, and I have the commemorative balls on display in my trophy room along with the tickets from the game that my wife kept.

Everything about Cal was class. He is the ultimate role model for everyone lucky enough to see him, whether major league player or sandlot hopeful. He played the game with so much talent and dignity. He was a guy I always respected and wanted to model myself after.

I'll never forget standing in right field that night as he was running down the line about 30 yards away, shaking hands. I probably should

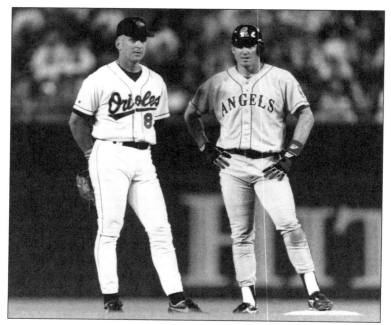

One of the classiest individuals and greatest competitors the game has ever known. Here, the great Cal Ripken shares a moment with me on his biggest night. Photo courtesy of the author

have gone over and shook his hand then myself, because nobody in the stadium on that amazing night held the man in greater awe than me.

The Nemesis

Randy Johnson

Every team has its nemesis, and throughout the 1990s, Seattle was ours. The Mariners were loaded with offensive weapons, guys who could really hurt you, but the one I flat-out dreaded was the pitching of Randy Johnson. "The Big Unit" was their ace, and he always kept us at bay. He was responsible for my all-time worst day, as well as for keeping us out of the playoffs in 1995.

The interesting thing about Randy is that, for a guy who was so intimidating and such a constant thorn in our side, he was actually a nice guy. Sometimes in the off-season we'd get together in Phoenix to play golf or go Jet Skiing. But once the season began, he acted as if he didn't even know me.

Stories abound about Randy emulating Nolan Ryan with his "throw a pitch under your grandma's chin" kind of mentality, were true enough when we played against him. But the next day he would be like, "Hey, Tim, let's hook up this winter!" *Wait a minute,* I'd think. *You're the guy grunting, snorting and looking all nasty, and now we're supposed to be friends?*

My first experience with Randy was during spring training in 1993. He had come over to Seattle from Montreal a few years earlier, and the book on him was that he had amazing potential but had yet to learn how to throw strikes. Getting ready to face him for the first time, I asked a veteran what he knew about Johnson.

"Shoot, he's easy," the veteran said. "Just go up to the plate and put your bat on your shoulder because he will never throw you a strike."

That sounded easy enough. I went up to the plate, and before I could blink, it was *zip-zip-zip*, and I was done. Three pitches, three strikes. The next time I got up it was the exact same thing: three pitches, three strikes. Suffice it to say, it wasn't anything close to the scouting report we got on him.

Just my luck, 1993 was the year he finally figured things out. He was almost untouchable after that. He'd throw 95 to 97 miles per hour in the days when 95 was considered absolute gas. Most guys who threw that hard were young and still stuck in Single or Double A, trying to figure it out. By the time they got to the big leagues, they had lost that velocity. Nowadays lots of young pitchers throw that hard or even harder, but back then only Johnson and maybe Roger Clemens, Troy Percival, and a few others could do it.

Randy's appearance itself was downright intimidating. He was tall with long hair, and by the time he released the ball it seemed as if he was right on top of you. My biggest concern was picking up his fastball early enough so that if it was headed anywhere near my head I could get out of the way. His big curve would also freeze you because you weren't used to seeing the ball come out from behind the second baseman's ear.

As tough as his curve and fastball were, it was Randy's slider that really gave me fits. It looked just like a fastball but had tremendous late movement. He'd throw it down and in and on your back foot. Even today you still see right-handed batters constantly checking their swing on it.

Players used to talk about him tipping his pitches, but I never felt comfortable trying to key in on something other than the ball. I had a hard enough time just trying to time his 96-miles-per-hour fastball. If I went to the plate guessing slider and was wrong, I might get clocked.

It was all a part of the Unit's psychological arsenal and one of the reasons he was so effective.

chapter 6

Swimming Upstream

Hitless in Seattle

Offensively, 1995 will go down as one the Angels' finest seasons. It seemed we could do whatever we wanted, almost scoring at will. Tony Phillips set the table with his great hitting eye drawing more than 100 walks, and with Jimmy Edmonds—having a breakout year—hitting in front of me, it seemed that someone was always in scoring position. I hit a career high .330 with 34 homers and 105 RBIs. Also wielding heavy bats behind me where Chili Davis, J.T. Snow, and rookie Garret Anderson. Our offensive production in the league was second only to the Cleveland Indians, who were starting their own winning tradition.

In early August we were 26 games over .500 and had an 11-game division lead. It looked as if the dreaded Angels curse had finally been broken. But, as they say, that's why you play the games. You have to play six months of good baseball to get in the postseason. We came out of the All-Star break playing decently, but we were also hearing lots of noise behind us. The Seattle Mariners were getting healthier and starting to play some good ball. Feeling pretty secure in our lead, we didn't give it much attention—at first.

Approaching the trade deadline, there was a lot of talk about acquiring David Cone from the Blue Jays. Every team coveted Cone, and Angels GM Bill Bavasi made trading for the Toronto ace (a prospective free agent the following year) his highest priority during the All-Star break. One of the league's best pitchers, the price tag was pretty hefty. I had heard that Toronto wanted our young flamethrower out of the pen, Troy Percival. Percy was a little too valuable in the minds of the management, so we passed on Coney and, taking our 11-game lead into consideration, traded for Jim Abbott of the White Sox. At that time, Coney was a true No. 1 starter and considered a definite difference-maker for any club going down the stretch. I remember a lot of the veterans saying, *You have to seize the opportunity at hand and make the deal.* But, I understood the tough position of management sitting on an 11-game lead thinking, *Why should we give up a Percival for this?* With the addition of Abbie, I think most of us felt that we had all the depth we would need.

Then Seattle went on a streak. Every night they were winning late in the game in spectacular fashion. *How were they going to do it tonight?* It finally caught our attention as our lead began to dwindle to eight…then six…then four. All of a sudden we caught ourselves really looking over our shoulders. It was late August and we had one losing stretch of nine in a row. Coming home for a crucial home stand against the East, the pressure was on. We faced a one-game makeup against Boston, three against New York, three more with Boston, and concluded with four against Baltimore. It was eerie how every team we faced had its 1-2-3 starters aligned to pitch in that homestand. It was a veritable buzzsaw of pitching that knocked us out of the division standings for good. Sure, we played well and had plenty of close games, but we lost eight of those 11 home games. Seattle took our spot in the driver's seat to a frenzy of national fanfare. They were the team with the amazing story and the team to watch the rest of the season. Randy Johnson had a Cy Young season on the mound, and Ken Griffey Jr. carried the offense down the stretch.

After allowing Seattle to put a few games between us, we improved in September. It was as if we had to finally face the embarrassing realization, *Yes, we did indeed just cough up the biggest lead in baseball history*. Once we accepted it, though, we were able to refocus our efforts and get back on track. Unfortunately, Seattle continued to play good ball. Heading into the final week of the season down two games to Seattle, we needed to sweep Oakland in a four-game series and get help from the Texas Rangers if we were going to win. Nothing short of a major miracle, it happened. We found ourselves deadlocked in a tie for first at the end of the season. It came down to a coin toss to see who would host the one-game playoff. I prayed that it would be Anaheim.

I knew we would face the soon-to-be-crowned Cy Young pitcher Randy Johnson. Over my career, my numbers were staggeringly better against him at home than in Seattle. In our bright, airy stadium at home, he didn't seem like he was standing on top of me. In fact, I'd done all right at home against the Big Unit; I even hit two home runs off of him. But in the enclosed Kingdome in Seattle, it was very different. The mound seemed closer there, making the 6'10" Johnson seem even more imposing. There, he seemed to strike me out at will.

Unfortunately, the toss didn't go our way. Hearing the news that we would be going to Seattle literally made me sick. But I convinced myself, *Things would be different this time*. I was coming off my best month of the season, raising my average to .332. Coming off a great series against Oakland, I really felt I was in a groove. We felt we had the momentum. Seattle was all packed and ready to meet the Yankees in the playoffs, and now they were coming home, possibly for good. This time it was the Angels who were making all the noise.

We figured the Mariners would be flat, but that all changed in the first inning when the Unit took the mound. The Kingdome was electric. I have never heard as much noise as I did that day. The fans finally had something to cheer about after all those losing seasons and they let it be known. Johnson came out firing bullets that looked like laser beams. Some of the veterans on the team mounted an attack a few times but it got snuffed out pretty quickly. The Unit seemed to elevate his pitching at will. I regret to say I was part of the rally killer. I struck out four times that day, including the final out of the game. I thought some of the strikes called against me were very questionable, if not downright awful. More than a few of us got victimized that day by a pretty liberal strike zone. Next time you see the highlight of Randy Johnson striking me out to end the game, pay attention to the last pitch thrown and you'll see what I mean. I'll admit that it is sour grapes on my part. I should have realized that when a superstar like Randy Johnson is throwing, strike zones get bigger. So either make an adjustment or take a seat. There's no use complaining.

Our season wasn't supposed to end like that. To battle all the way back like we did, it seemed as if destiny was going to be on our side. After the game, everyone in the locker room was crushed. I was as depressed as I'd ever been. I had a great season personally, but when it mattered most to the team, I tanked four times in a row. It still nags me to this day.

People still ask me what happened that year. There is never an easy answer. Baseball is a team game, and everyone has some responsibility for the collapse. But I do still wonder what might have happened if we had traded for David Cone. Having him on the mound every fifth day, I can't imagine that we could have lost nine games in a row—twice! Even without him, we still managed to get back into it and tie Seattle at the end of the year. Just one win by him could have made the difference. I can understand now what some of the veterans were alluding to, talking about trade deadline deals. When you feel you have the team to take you all the way, you don't pass on someone like a David Cone who can really put you over the top. Looking back on the whole trade deal, it would have been hard to see Troy Percival having all his success in a Toronto uniform. The only reason I can live with the nightmare of 1995 today is because of this: the no-deal paid big dividends for us later on, as Percy secured our first world championship in 2002.

The Learning Years

Looking back at my most productive seasons, what immediately comes to mind are all the times I'd walk up to the plate, look toward third base, and see Jimmy Edmonds, Darin Erstad, or Tony Phillips standing there looking back at me. It's a fact that when there are men on base, you tend to get better pitches to hit. They were on base all the time and the successes I achieved in 1995 and '97 are directly related to the talent hitting around me. Those were fun years for me offensively. The Angels had teams that could flat-out hit and I always found myself right in the middle of those lineups. Every season has its ups and downs, but looking back I don't recall ever going through extended slumps. We might have had issues with pitching depth, but our offensive depth kept us in the hunt through the summer.

I always felt that if we just kept slugging away, winning would take care of itself. But as we continually faded down the stretch each season, I realized it wasn't enough. *Winning pennants*, I realized, *comes down to pitching*. As the long season winds down in September, fatigue sets in on hitters, slowing down offensive production. Pitching depth down the stretch is vitally more important than hitting. Trying to outslug your opponent is a tough task to accomplish night after night, month after month.

For a variety of reasons, this is often the position our clubs were in. And of course, we had the dreaded Angels curse to deal with as well. Every year the question seemed to be, *How are we going to slide out of contention this year?* I guess history gave some credence to the thought, but each year we as a team were bound and determined that this time would be different. As much as we wanted to reject the curse, I have to admit there *was* some strangeness going on. Take 1997 for example: a lot of weird things happened down the stretch. One of our horses on the pitching staff, Chuck Finley, broke his wrist while backing up a play at home plate. Losing our stud pitcher for the remainder of the season was bad enough. But then, on the very next play, our young, hot-hitting catcher, Todd Greene, got injured on a foul tip. He was side-lined as well. That's just one example of how snake-bit we seemed during some pretty good campaigns during the '90s.

My philosophy on winning changed over time when I began to see what depth could do for an organization. As new management crystallized around the 2000 season, you could see an emphasis being put on scouting, drafting, and developing depth at key positions like pitching. Although hitting always seems to be on the market, getting quality pitching is harder to come by. The Angels' minor-league clubs began to bolster themselves with a stable of quality arms who could be called upon by the big club when needed. This depth contributed to strong bullpens in Anaheim that really took the pressure off the hitters. There's no better example than in 2002. We had a solid rotation that consistently gave us six or seven solid innings a game. When the starters turned it over to the bullpen, it was usually lights out. Then, when Frankie Rodriguez was tapped from the minor leagues late that year, we became unstoppable. With our bullpen that year, any late-inning leads that year were pretty secure. I remember standing in the outfield at one time and think-ing, *Shoot, these games are getting really short!*

As I look back on the teams of the '90s, I can see more clearly what kept us from winning down the stretch. Maybe it wasn't so much the fate of the Gods or bad luck or a curse. We had great talent in a lot of positions, but we just weren't deep enough. We had to roll the dice and hope everyone stayed healthy for us to win. I learned a lot of valuable lessons in those lost years from 1995 to 2000. Many

In the mid-'90s, I played in an outfield with some of the league's very best, Jim Edmonds (left) and Garret Anderson (center).

of them were about losing late in the season. But that's what made the winning years to come that much sweeter.

Reality Check

"Baseball is just a game." I don't know how many times I have heard that comment. It is a difficult notion to live with sometimes when you are grinding it out day after day in the big leagues. In 1997, something happened that changed my understanding of the game for good. My wife Marci was diagnosed with thyroid cancer, and the words hit me harder than any fastball to the face. Anyone who has ever been to the doctor and heard the words "cancer" and a loved one's name in the same sentence knows what I mean. It's a punch to the gut that literally makes you sick. I was 28 years old, with a young child, and I just been broadsided by the most dreaded word in the English language. And now I was supposed to go out and play baseball?

We were scheduled to play at home against the Seattle Mariners that day, and word spread throughout the clubhouse by the time I arrived, late. My teammates were shocked to see me. "Marci wants me here," I told them. "She feels my being here for a few hours is best for both of us, and that it'll get my mind off of things." That night I barely acknowledged that I was playing a baseball game. I approached my duties with an indifference I have never experienced—at any level of play. I couldn't have cared less about anything going on around me. Honestly, I shouldn't have been in the game with that kind of attitude. It was a selfish desire to be out there, a vain hope I could somehow heal the wounds of the news I had heard. The news spread to the crowd about Marci's diagnosis, and each time my name was announced I got a louder-than-usual cheer. When I came up to bat in the eighth inning with the bases loaded in a tight game, I hit a bases-clearing double that put us ahead. The fans went crazy.

Everyone must have thought that I somehow rose to the occasion, bolstered by my recent news. But standing on second base, I knew differently. I was totally going through the motions. Why was the crowd acting like this was the most important thing in life? Who cares that I just batted in the game-winning runs? I have to wake up to a new reality tomorrow.

That's when it really hit me like a lightning bolt. Baseball was fun, and it provided me with a very good living, but it was still just a game. Marci's cancer was a wake-up call that I answered right there on second base. There is nothing more important than the people we love. Baseball had always been the central focus of my life, but I realized then that if I never played another game, my life would still be rich and full, thanks to my family. Without my wife's health, nothing else mattered.

Surgeons removed her thyroid, and after a few months of radiation therapy, she was cancer-free. But her experience will remain in the back of my mind, especially when she goes in for her annual "well checks." It takes a special woman to be a baseball player's wife. I think about all of the single guys searching for a spouse and hope they all end up as lucky as me. I honestly think that a strong, healthy marriage is a necessary component of success in baseball or any other career.

Along with being a great wife and mother, Marci was also my best hitting coach. She knew more about my swing and my struggles than anyone. To come home after a rough game to someone who knew exactly what I was going through was a blessing. I could tell her things I couldn't even share with my teammates. To have someone to whom can reveal your heart and soul is huge. There's a great deal of healing that comes from that, and it got me through many a long season. Without Marci's love and support, none of my success in baseball would have been possible. And I can say for certain that none of it would have been worthwhile.

The Catch

Jim Edmonds

I've known Jimmy Edmonds a long time. We were roommates in Palm Springs Class A ball in 1990. He is one of the nicest guys you'd ever want to meet. Jimmy was fearless on the field, always exuding the self-confidence of a seasoned vet. Once, on an off day for us in Palm Springs, Jimmy, Marci, Dave Partrick, and I piled into a car and took off for Anaheim Stadium to watch a major-league game. It was after my beaning injury, and my jaw was wired shut. As a result, I could eat only food that had been pureed to the consistency of baby food. All the way from Palm Springs to Anaheim I sat there cradling a little ice chest, sucking down blended concoctions and driving everybody nuts with my loud slurping.

The first time in a big-league clubhouse can be intimidating for any minor leaguer. After a brief introductory tour by then-manager Doug Rader, we headed to the Angels' bench and did our best to stay out of everybody's way. Watching batting practice for the first time in Anaheim Stadium was awesome. The Angels were playing the Kansas City Royals, and as the visiting team emerged from the opposite dugout for their pregame warm-ups.

"Look, there goes Willie Wilson! And Frank White! Oh my gosh, there's George Brett over there!"

Jimmy was just as starstruck as us, but he wasn't going sit there with his tongue hanging out. I heard him say, "Wow, George Brett! I gotta go talk to him," and there went Edmonds trotting off toward the Royals dugout. If my jaw hadn't been wired shut, my chin would have bounced off the dugout floor. "Dude!" I hissed at Jimmy's departing back. "You can't just go over there and talk to George Brett!" But that's exactly what he did, and after introducing himself to the Royals' star third-baseman, Edmonds and Brett spent the next 20 minutes yakking like long-lost brothers. We couldn't believe it. "Does George even know who he is?" I asked Dave incredulously.

Jimmy was never afraid of doing the unconventional thing. He'd decided that he was going to talk to George Brett, and without giving it another thought, that's just what he did. Brett could've looked at this brash kid and just blown him off, but apparently he liked Jimmy's chutzpah. Some other ballplayers did not. As a rookie in the big leagues, when Edmonds hit a home run he would strut around the bases hooting, hollering, and doing everything but turning cartwheels. Nowadays that's almost standard operating procedure, but back then that kind of behavior was strictly taboo, especially for a rookie. But Jimmy, one of the original if-it-feels-good-do-it guys, couldn't have cared less what anybody else thought.

His antics not only drove other teams nuts but sometimes his own teammates. On a few occasions I screamed at Jimmy to run, instead of standing there staring at his home runs. From a purely selfish standpoint, I sometimes wished Jimmy kept it down to a small roar. As the guy who batted right behind him in the lineup, I ended up paying for his sins more than once at the hands of a smoldering pitcher with retaliation on his mind. Once, after Jimmy hit a home run off Cleveland's Julian Tavarez and started pimping around the base paths, I stood there in the on-deck circle watching the steam blow out of Tavarez's ears. Jimmy always hit especially well against Cleveland—he absolutely crushed them for some reason—and I remember some of the Indians grousing to us as he went into his act. "What's with this guy? He can't be doing that!" We just shrugged helplessly and sheepishly told them, "Well, Jimmy's really a nice guy, but he just does some things a little differently, that's all."

Outside of Kenny Lofton, Jimmy was probably the best center fielder in baseball. He didn't have blazing speed like Lofton, but he made up for it with lots of intangibles plus an uncanny sense of where to position himself. He had a knack for making acrobatic catches and incredible dives. Jimmy had eagle eyes and claimed he could see the catcher putting down the signs for the pitcher. Whether that was the case or it was just his ability to anticipate where the ball would go, he always seemed to be in the right spot to haul it in.

One of my greatest memories is of Edmonds making what many still say was one of the finest catches ever made. And I had a closer look at it than anybody else. It happened on June 10, 1997, at Kauffman Stadium in Kansas City. The batter was David Howard, whose average momentarily rose in the fifth inning when he got a

In 1997 I had a bird's-eye view of one of baseball's all-time great catches. To this day, I still can't believe Jim Edmonds caught that ball. Photo courtesy of AP Images

hold of one and launched it to deep center. Because Howard wasn't known for his power, Jimmy was playing him really shallow, within spitting distance of second base. As soon as Howard made contact, I started sprinting toward the center-field wall screaming, "Back, back, back," figuring there was no way Jimmy could play the ball if it stayed in the park. But all of a sudden there he was, running full tilt toward the fence, with his back to the ball. Arching his head upward he strained to keep his eyes on the arcing baseball. Just as I was about to yell "Wall!" to warn him of his impending death, Jimmy left his feet diving headfirst toward the warning track. Fully extended, he somehow caught the ball like a wide receiver.

It was absolutely amazing. It felt as if he had made a game-saving catch but it was only the fifth inning. I sprinted over to congratulate him thinking, *He made the catch! I can't believe he made the catch!* Jimmy was sprawled out on the ground when I got to him. I probably didn't do him any good standing over him and screaming "Way to go!" but I was so excited by what he'd done that I even forgot we were in the middle of a ballgame.

When the magnitude of the catch sunk in, I figured that because we were playing in Kansas City it wouldn't get much media coverage. Fortunately for Jimmy, the media jumped all over it and gave him due credit. You'd have to look up the final score, because I've forgotten it, but I won't ever forget that stunning catch by Jimmy Edmonds that cemented his status as a Gold Glove center fielder.

In spring 2002, Jimmy was traded to St. Louis for Adam Kennedy and Kent Bottenfield. He'd gotten banged up a bit, and with new management coming in they felt he was a necessary move to tighten up other areas of team. Jimmy went on to have some career years with the Cardinals, and we didn't fare so badly either. That same Adam Kennedy ended up being the hero in our American League championship-clinching game.

Watching the one-man band that was Jimmy Edmonds was unquestionably one of my greatest thrills in baseball. He was one of the most talented players I had ever run across in the game. It was a real privilege to play alongside him and watch him make some amazing catches while he was with the Angels.

Clubhouse Cop

Troy Percival

If there was one guy on the Angels who demanded accountability in the clubhouse, it was Troy Percival. He was truly a vocal leader in every sense. Anytime something needed attention, he confronted it head-on, usually in a booming voice that didn't get much rebuttal. Percy had a wit to him that would catch people off guard as well. A naturally funny guy, he would usually be in the back of the bus making light of an otherwise sensitive situation. His approach either lightened the tensions of the moment or raised issue with something that needed to be brought to the forefront.

Percy didn't have too many issues with me. I think he respected me in my own right for what I did on and off the field. I was an occasional target for him when he tried to get me out of Timmy Land. I was guilty as charged more then a few times.

As a veteran leader on the team, I probably didn't take notice of some of the issues around the clubhouse. On a typical day, my drive to the ballpark was filled with mental preparation and the schedule I needed to keep before the game. As soon as I stepped out of my car, I was already in deep concentration about everything I had to check off my list. I'd walk right by people on my way to my locker without taking much notice.

Perched at a card table in the middle of the clubhouse, Percy would yell, "Hey, Fish! How you doing today? Where did you go to lunch?" He couldn't have cared less about my answer, just as long as

I gave him one. He was onto my game and felt he was doing his part to draw me back into the fold. Looking back on it from a different perspective, I can understand the motive behind his annoying attempts. It did bring me out of Timmy Land, if only for a few moments. More important, it served as a reminder to me that communication is an important aspect of team chemistry. It was different after we took the field. When the game started, Timmy Land was exactly where Percy wanted me to be, oblivious to everything but the game and playing to the best of my abilities.

Troy and I didn't see eye to eye on everything, but I still think that we had the kind of bond you see in families. We may not agree with each other, but at the end of the day there is too much water under the bridge to not support one another. We have opposite personalities. I was low key while he was loud and in the middle of every conversation. We weren't ever going to become best buddies, but we knew where each other stood and we mutually respected one another.

Percy made it his business to be sure that everything operated the way a big-league clubhouse should. It is an old-school philosophy that you don't see much of today. The Tampa Bay Rays tapped into some of this philosophy when Joe Maddon gave Percy the closer role a few years ago. It must have worked, because in 2008 the Rays made it to the World Series with a bunch of youngsters. Players with that kind of influence are hard to find. During his career, Percy's leadership style made the difference for two organizations in his career, and I was lucky to be on one of them.

Transition

When I first made my appearance in Anaheim in 1992, the Angels were a family-run team. We probably had the most famous owner of any in professional sports, and I have to admit that playing for Gene Autry was pretty cool. I can still remember how excited my dad was that I got to

Mr. Autry was an inspirational owner and an integral figure in Angels history.

meet his childhood hero, the Singing Cowboy. My dad told me stories of all the collectibles he had as a kid. One day when visiting my grandmother's house in Long Beach, I made a trip to the garage and pulled out my dad's keepsake trunk. There it was, a treasure trove of Gene Autry comic books. As I leafed through them, I began to form a new appreciation for the man behind the stories. Gene Autry was every boy's hero in the 1950s, and I started to realize why. One day I brought a few of the comic books to the stadium with the intention of getting an autograph or two from Mr. Autry. I mentioned that I wanted to surprise my dad with them and Mr. Autry suggested I *really* surprise him by having Dad sit in the owner's luxury box with him for a game. To say my dad was ecstatic is a huge understatement. My dad took all his comic books with him and Mr. Autry went through each book sharing insight on each and every storyline. I still wonder if that evening was the biggest highlight of my career in my dad's mind.

When the Autrys owned the Angels, it was very much a family business. The front office consisted of longtime friends and there was a sense of loyalty to the man at the top. That era was slowly coming to an end, though. For the Angels, Mr. Autry was getting pretty old and I guess they reasoned it was time to pass on the torch to someone younger and more capable of running the team. In stepped the competition down the street in Disney.

When Disney took over in 1997, everything seemed to change. I have to say, it was a shot in the arm, initially. There was an excitement and anticipation at all levels of the organization as to what was next. There was a flurry of rumors, some of them plausible and some of them far-fetched. One even promised that a monorail was going to be built to connect the stadium to Disneyland. I became an instant hit with my kids when I told them I was working for Mickey Mouse. And Mickey Mouse it was, as Disney began testing a variety of entertainment ideas inside the stadium. They wanted excitement, color, and lots of hoopla. By the end of that first season we had "Angel Wings" (cheerleaders) perched behind the outfield fence. The change was not wildly popular among the players. In our minds, baseball was supposed to be old school and most of us were a little shocked at the attempt to change the culture, but the trend was already taking root in other sports, such as the NBA and the NFL, with pretty good success. I guess it was inevitable and as you'd expect it was Disney blazing the trail in the major leagues.

With exception of Mickey Mouse and team president Tony Tavares, the Disney people were practically invisible. In fact, Tavares was actually the only Disney executive I ever saw around. I never saw CEO Michael Eisner until the celebration after our 2002 World Series win. I made it a point to shower him with champagne as a nice-to-finally-meet-you-welcome-to-the-clubhouse gesture.

It was clearly evident that there was a new entity making the decisions from the top. The bureaucracy that you'd expect from a major corporation became a burr in the saddle of many Angels employees. Jobs were reassigned or consolidated with the Anaheim Ducks' front office in an attempt to streamline operations between the two teams. On paper it might have made sense to executives, but to those involved in the everyday operations of the club, it was an unwelcome change. But that's the way it goes with a corporate takeover.

It's easy to focus on Disney's shortcomings, but they also had some pretty impressive accomplishments as well. Signing Mo Vaughn demonstrated that we now had the resources to get necessary pieces of the puzzle that we couldn't get in the past. Mo may not have helped us win the World Series directly, but trading him for Kevin Appier certainly did. And it was under Disney's reign that former Dodgers catcher Mike Scioscia and general manager Bill Stoneman came aboard.

We won our first world championship under its ownership and Disney deserves much of the credit for it. When the following season rolled along, Disney promptly capitalized on the new value of its investment and sold the Angels to Arte Moreno. I am thankful for the benefits that came from the Disney ownership, including the annual Silver Pass that got my family into Disneyland free of charge. We got our money's worth, for sure, and it provided so many great memories for my kids.

"Fish Grease"

Mo Vaughn

The Cape Cod baseball summer program is an invitation-only league. The competition features some of the best players in the nation showing off their abilities to play in a wooden-bat environment. Every year, most of the top picks from the amateur draft are selected from this league. It was in this league, way back in 1988, where I first met Mo Vaughn. Representing his alma mater, Seton Hall, Mo had a presence about him when he stepped onto the field, even back then. Our first introduction came by way of a collision at first base, when I was trying to leg out an infield hit. He was already a big guy back then but I somehow managed to survive. Mo was one of the premier players destined for big leagues, and those predictions were right on when he went on to star for the Boston Red Sox, earning an MVP Award.

Mo was a gregarious, larger-than-life figure who had a nickname for everyone. It was his way showing his acceptance of you and bringing the team together. For some unexplained reason, my nickname was "Fish Grease." The "Fish" part I get, but I'm still trying to figure out where "Grease" came from. I never did get an answer that made any sense, but everyone seemed to enjoy the odd combination of verbiage, so it stuck.

Mo had a leadership quality about him that screamed, *The buck stops here*. Never shying away from an opportunity to hold court with the media, his days in Boston provided a great training ground in dealing with them. Truly a superstar, he embraced everything that came with it. There was no bigger threat in baseball than Mo up to bat with the game on the line. He was one of those rare players who shined whenever the spotlight was on him. For years I got to see those heroics from my vantage point in right field. All that changed in 1999 when he donned an Angels jersey and he hit in front of me in the order. Then I had the best seat in the house to see him take his ferocious cuts and inflicting damage on all our opponents.

Mo arrived in Southern California with a big splash. A perennial All-Star in Boston, his big bat was expected to put the Angels over the hump. But it didn't happen as planned. On Opening Day that season, Mo was tracking a routine foul ball by Cleveland's Omar Vizquel when he hit the top step of the visitors' dugout and fell in. He sprained his ankle and badly bruised the bone, and the injury just about killed our season. It never healed completely and slowed Mo down to the point that he became a liability on defense and the base paths.

Hitting behind him in the lineup, his slowed mobility had its effect on me. In 2000 I ended the season with 97 RBIs, and the following year in spring training Mo was riding me hard about it. "Fish Grease," he said, "you couldn't get three more lousy RBIs?"

"Mo," I responded, "if I had anybody else in the world but you running in front of me, I would have had at least 120 and probably a dozen more extra-base hits."

I've had similar injuries, so I know what he went through playing on a bum ankle. In '99, Mo still managed to hit 33 home runs with 108 RBIs—and led the team in both categories—but his injury took a heavy toll. Compensating it probably caused him to use more of his upper body, which resulted in a torn bicep tendon. This injury caused him to miss the entire 2001 season.

Mo was a fun-loving guy who unfortunately got caught up in a difficult transitional period. His years with us, 1999 to 2001, were tough ones. In '99, a lot freaky things happened to the team in addition to Mo's injury. Jimmy Edmonds, Disar, Fin, and I all got hurt that season. Throw in a volatile coaching staff and the situation was grim from every angle. Looking back on that 1999 team, I cannot believe how much our attitudes changed from the optimism of spring training to the end of the season. Between the injuries and firings, it was definitely a year to forget.

Mo was eventually traded to the New York Mets for Kevin Appier in 2002. This move brought us some much-needed help on the mound and opened the door at first base for a future World Series hero Scott Spiezio. So in a way he did help us get the ultimate prize.

I have nothing but respect for Mo Vaughn. He was a talented guy who raised the level of play of everyone around him. He was a leader and a difference-maker on the field. He also had a big heart and fun spirit. He was with us for only a few seasons, but I always smile when I think about his those crazy nicknames—and I'm still scratching my head about mine.

chapter 7

Final Pieces of the Puzzle

Thinking Outside the Box

Mike Scioscia

When people ask me about Mike Scioscia, the first thing I say is that he runs a great clubhouse. The atmosphere is so conducive to winning; it is unlike any I have ever experienced. From the player personnel to the coaches on his staff, it all seems to jell inside the inner confines of the ballpark. Make no mistake, it is all a part of his master plan. Every spring the seeds of team chemistry are sown in what most players would say is the best-run training camp in the game. Just about anyone new to the Angels comments on how much fun that morning meeting is and how it sets the tone for the day's work. Scioscia creates a mood of excitement that really builds team unity and camaraderie.

My favorite memory of Scioscia occurred in one such spring-training morning meeting. But first I have to give some background about the situation. Sosh is big on player introductions and getting to know some of the new or younger guys on the team. Humor is usually the icebreaker, and a player's ability to play along with it is key. Often a player's favorite hobby or activity provides the fodder necessary for his

One of the great minds in the game today, Mike Scioscia has provided the Angels with the much needed stability every winning franchise needs.

comic genius. Typically, the result will be a "project" for the player to bring back to the team meeting on a later date. To use an example, a player from Texas, John Lackey's home state, might be required to put together a chart featuring all the current Angels players from Texas and any pertinent information about them. Sosh usually finds a way to make the situation hilarious.

He is a prankster—and he won't get bent out of shape when the joke's on him. One spring training, Sosh dispatched a couple rookies to the local renaissance fair. Their assignment was to give an investigative report and videotape the medieval festivities for the team. Unbeknownst to Sosh, the rookies had a little support from some of the veterans, looking to turn the tables on the manager. Taking one of Sosh's jerseys with them, these guys were able to recruit a renaissance actor to team up with them in their ploy. The actor weighed about 350 pounds and sported long hair and a shaggy beard. Squeezing him into Sosh's jersey, they made sure he was in the background of every scene, doing subtle but weird things. During a sword-swallower demonstration, the 350-pound behemoth was in the background simulating the feat with a turkey leg bigger than a Louisville Slugger. The background effect wasn't noticed immediately, but when it was, it was priceless. There were several similar scenes, and as the video ran, everybody picked up on it—except for one person. Sosh was oblivious that the joke was on him. The final shot featured Shakespearean actors performing in front of a giant Trojan rocking horse. After several moments the camera gradually panned up the rocking horse, and the huge guy in the Scioscia jersey was rocking away on it like a little kid, and yelling "Wheeeeee!"

After the roar of laughter, Sosh demanded to know what was so funny. When his hefty screen counterpart was pointed out wearing his jersey, nobody laughed harder than Sosh. In fact the tape was rewound so Sosh could see what he had been missing out on all along. Seeing Mike's hysterical response was almost as funny as the video. You can learn a lot about people who can laugh at themselves.

When the Angels hired Mike Scioscia as manager in 2000, there were some questions about what they were getting in a rookie manager. The previous coaching staff had been cleaned out from top to bottom, so Scioscia had to come in and fix the mess. Names like Jim Fregosi and other veteran managers had been thrown around, so I was a little bit surprised when they went with a first-time manager. As history would have it, he ended up being the wise choice. He gave the team a transfusion of Dodgers blood: the tradition of excellence, the philosophy of doing things right from top to bottom.

Love or hate them, the Dodgers have always played a style of ball that includes manufacturing runs and a reliance on great pitching and defense. An emphasis on stable pitching and sound defensive play was ingrained in Scioscia, and he brought it with him across town to Anaheim. He figured that with the right kind of hitters, runs can be manufactured, but good pitching and defense are mainstays that require constant emphasis. The Angels, on the other hand, had enjoyed some great offensive clubs and solid defenses, but holes in pitching were a constant problem. From day one, the manager's main focus was pitching and defense.

One reason Mike is such a successful manager is his preparation. With the help of his coaching staff, there is not one aspect of the game that is overlooked. A master planner, he has every conceivable drill, scenario, and option available to him covered by the time he gets to spring training. In the last couple of years I've had the privilege of sitting in Mike's spring-training staff meetings. I have always come away impressed with his sound input in every facet of team preparation. He is a micromanager at times, but it is because he understands what needs to be done in every aspect of the game. This is the reason he's rarely caught off guard. He has planned for every possible scenario far in advance.

Mike was a gritty, hard-nosed player in his day and understands what players respond to. He also possesses a sophisticated understanding of the game. It is in the finer points of the game where he is most impressive. Countless times I have passed by his office and seen him sitting at his desk scouring the stat sheets or reading the MLB rules handbook. He analyzes complex numbers and on-base percentages, thinking beyond the box and translating it into a game-day strategy. He can break down these 21st-century stats like very few other managers can.

And how about all the times Sosh runs on the field to argue a call? Those poor umpires are in for an education. I guarantee you that he knows more about the rules in the book than most of those umpires do. Often you will see Sosh question the most innocuous play and think there can't possibly be anything to argue about. But trust me, he is always looking to stretch the boundaries of the rulebook, taking advantage of any gray area that might benefit him. On the rare occasions when he is wrong, you can find him after the game, flipping through his worn-out rulebook and looking for a loophole.

He is consistently able to see the whole picture. The game is not a sprint but a marathon, and that concept is central to his managerial decision-making. Many times managers get caught up in the mindset of *Win today and worry about tomorrow when it comes*. If this is done without planning and discretion, it can cause all kinds of problems over the course of a season.

While winning is always a priority, Sosh isn't afraid to rest a key player or hold off rushing someone back from the DL in favor of guaranteeing his long-term health and production. It is his patience and perspective that keep him from making rash decisions. Sure, it helps to have a deep bench or good minor league talent from which to draw, but those are other aspects of his preparedness. Coming out of spring training, he knows exactly which players can help him on the bench or in the minors, and he makes sure that they are ready to contribute when called upon. It is a message that is heard loud and clear throughout the organization: *Be ready, because he's not afraid to use you if needed.*

Most people don't know that Sosh is a bit of a master psychologist. Just ask any player or newspaper reporter who has sat on his couch in his office. Anyone who has been on that couch usually finds himself walking out the door having agreed to something but not exactly sure what it is they agreed to or why. It is Sosh's unique ability to sway just about anyone to his position. I can't tell you how many times I walked into his office determined to do one thing and came out wondering how I'd just been talked into doing just the opposite. Many a player has stormed into his office hell-bent on rejecting a day off only to leave his office convinced that he probably could use one. The man has a golden tongue.

As a motivator, he's in touch with the inner workings of his personnel, and he knows what makes them tick. Part of his process involves breaking down the old-school barriers that kept the veterans and the rookies in their "proper" places. Under Sosh, the playing field is level—and that includes the clubhouse. Egos are checked at the locker room door. Young guys still need to rely on the veteran leadership, but they need to know they are respected and accountable for doing their part, just like the veterans. Having that comfort level is something that has helped build team unity and chemistry.

I believe it is a combination of all these attributes that provided what the Angels organization needed to get over the hump and win our first-ever world championship in 2002. Mike's focus on the little things leaves nothing to fall between the cracks. His mantra of "one game at a time, one inning, one at-bat, one pitch," has narrowed everyone's approach down to the smallest controllable detail. His managerial prowess is no better bolstered than by the fact that two of his former coaches are now big-league managers. I'm sure there will be more to come as organizations seek to tap into his methodologies and pluck those disciples out from under him.

Sosh's influence has not gone unnoticed by me. I have had the opportunity to be around him as a player and now in retirement as a guest coach in spring training. As I become more involved in my own kids' lives, coaching their Little League teams, I often find myself quoting Sosh's mantras to the kids. Managerial trends are part of all professional sports. Every decade or so, someone comes up with a new style of coaching that sets a new trend. Without a doubt, the Angels were lucky to land a manager like Mike Scioscia and get on the front end of that wave. I'm convinced that when it is all said and done, he will go down as not only one of the all-time great managers in Angels history but in the history of the game as well.

Renaissance Man
Joe Maddon

When you start singling out the people most responsible for your success, you run the risk of leaving out one or two who deserve as much credit as anybody else. I've had a lot of help over the years, but of all the guys who really had a big impact on me, Joe Maddon has to be the most influential.

Joe is the most positive individual I've ever run across. As much I'd like to think our relationship is unique, I have to believe that just about everybody he has come in contact with probably feels the same way. Back when I was with him in the minor leagues, it seemed as if he'd been in the minors forever and that he had influenced the careers of so many before me. Today, as a big-league manager, you would hardly know he had such a long minors career.

I think that the main reason Joe is so popular is that he has a genuine respect for people and is extremely well rounded. Too often with baseball people it's all baseball, all the time; bring up something unrelated to the sport and they're a fish out of water. Not Joe. He's up to speed on everything. Whether it's politics, world history, the latest great book or TV show, Joe brings an educated opinion to the table. I'm not a bit surprised

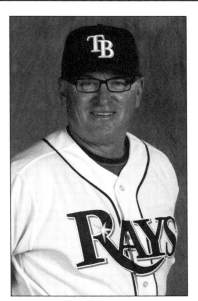

Joe Maddon was unequivocally one of the most influential people in my baseball career.
Photo courtesy of Tampa Bay Rays/Erik Ruiz

by where he is now in his career and the success he's had in Tampa. He's baseball's renaissance man, a guy destined for great things.

Just like Mike Scioscia, Joe is very much a student of the game. His ability to evaluate the game's intricacies as they happen keeps him ahead of the curve in a lot of things. When he was a member of Sosh's staff, it was hard to know who was influencing who sometimes. Both men are ardent intellectuals, and they honed their success at the same time, though Joe's happened to be behind the scenes. Over the years he and Sosh have developed a winning philosophy. It's a work in progress really, but they've collaborated on the same things and that's the main reason both are succeeding similarly.

I've always appreciated Joe and the influence he had on my career. There's always that special coach, person, or teammate who helps gets you through the rough times, and for me it was him. I could always interrupt him at his computer desk if I needed to get a shot of confidence. If you listened close enough you might learn something profound as well. Because Joe was with me for the bulk of my career, I have no problem identifying him as the one who influenced me the most.

Unsung Hero

Billy Bavasi

I was lucky to have some terrific guys in my corner during my career, like Joe Maddon and Billy Bavasi. Billy's influence on me was as valuable as Joe's. He was head of the Angels' minor league operation when I first joined the organization in '89, and in a way our careers traveled parallel paths. We both went through the system at the same time, and we kind of grew up together.

We formed our special relationship in the minor leagues. After getting the news of my horrendous beaning in Palm Springs in 1989, Billy's encouragement and support was instrumental in helping me get back on my feet. Throughout that ordeal, Billy always seemed more concerned about me as a person then as a player. Whatever it took for me to get better was fine with him. If it turned out I couldn't play anymore, he was all for me coming back to the organization in whatever capacity I could. My wife and I are convinced he would have done anything for me to get back on track, and for that we are forever grateful.

When I first got called up to the Angels, the GM was Whitey Herzog. I didn't know him personally, and I was massively intimidated. When Billy took over for Herzog in 1994 it was a real blessing for me. After I got off to my (typically) slow start that season, some members of the media started getting on Billy about it. His response was swift and to the point: "You know what, guys? I know about Timmy, and he's the one guy you don't have to worry about. I've known him long enough to know that he's going to be where he needs to be. He's just a slow starter, so don't worry."

To get that kind of a backing from a GM when you're really struggling is an incredible boost. Most players are always concerned about what the GM and coaches are thinking, but I didn't have to worry about that with Billy and Joe Maddon. There was always a comfort level with them.

Billy was instrumental in holding on to the essential core of players that turned the Angels into contenders. Personally, I don't think he gets enough credit for constructing the 2002 championship team. Jimmy Edmonds, Chad Curtis, Gary DiSarcina, J.T. Snow, and Mo Vaughn weren't on the World Series team, but each was part of the nucleus of players that got the Angels organization headed in the right direction. Although they were eventually traded, those players he brought in were the ones who helped us reach the summit. It's too bad Billy wasn't around when we won the championship because you can find his fingerprints all over that World Series trophy.

Ersty and Eck

Darin Erstad and David Eckstein

If I sit back and think to myself, *Who would I trust the most to catch the last out in Game 7 of a World Series?*, without a doubt it would be the man who caught it for us in 2002. There is not another player who I could say that about with the confidence I have in Darin Erstad. Period. From the first day I met him in spring training back in 1996 I knew he was different than most other bonus babies. Ersty had a no-nonsense attitude about him even back then. It was refreshing to see, especially since he would be hanging out with me in the outfield.

With his blond hair, light skin, and Northern accent, he seemed more like a choirboy than a future team leader and Gold Glover. He didn't talk much at all; we probably exchanged all of three words the entire spring. But I was impressed by the way he carried himself as a rookie. He listened more than he spoke and always worked his tail off. Eventually he was sent down to the minor league camp, but he had left the right impression with everyone. His hard work eventually paid off, and in only his second professional season he was called up from Triple A Vancouver on a couple of occasions.

When I learned he had been a punter at the University of Nebraska, we started talking football, and our friendship was cemented thereafter. Like the days of throwing pass patterns with my brother Mike, the following spring I found myself staying after workouts to throw them with Darin. One particular day we threw pass patterns for an hour and a half. Something about the adrenaline pumping through you makes common sense go out the window. The next day I could hardly lift my arm, and for the rest of camp it was painful to even throw a baseball. Having developed a slight case of tendinitis, it was all I could do to nurse it before the season started.

Ersty's style of play made him our balls-to-the-wall team leader. Always a maximum-effort player, his hard-nosed play got him the dirtiest uniform after every game, and he always seemed to end up bleeding, too. When he left it all on the field, he left that and more. Hitting behind him for the better part of my career, I saw firsthand the difference he made. Always a patient hitter, he knew how to work an at-bat to his favor and then hit a laser with that quick swing of his. I always appreciated his approach, because it allowed me the timing and rhythm I needed on deck, not to mention that it stressed the

Darin Erstad's all-out play and intensity inspired everyone. A leader by example, he brought everyone around him to a higher level.

pitcher before I even got there. When on base, he was as good as they come running the bases. If he wasn't stealing second, scoring from first was no problem for him on an extra-base hit. His aggressive play set an example for the rest of the team and made us all better.

Like the rest of us, Ersty had his own set of quirky routines that further defined him. He seemed to make it a point to always be the first to arrive and the last to leave the clubhouse. Often, he'd be waiting at the clubhouse door for Ken Higdon, the clubhouse manager, to unlock it. Adhering to a strict personal schedule, the possibility of the slightest deviation from it was enough to stress him out.

There was never a better teammate or person than David Eckstein. Photo courtesy of Getty Images

The first time I invited him out to lunch as a rookie we were in New York. "I don't know, Fish," he said reluctantly, like I'd asked him to go bungee jumping off the Empire State Building. I assured him we would be at the stadium in time for early hitting. I was thinking like 15 minutes early, not an hour and a half early. The whole time we were eating he was fidgeting, checking his watch. Looking back on it, he was probably worried about how he could eat and run without showing a lack of respect to a veteran. I had no clue at the time that he was so fanatical about his schedule, but I would soon find out. And I don't believe we ever shared a pregame meal together again.

Ersty's style of play and personality made him a solid team leader, and it was well deserved. He let his actions on the field speak for him, most of the time. At team meetings Ersty generally didn't say much, but if he had a gripe, he didn't hold back. He liked to call them like he saw them, so any attempts to sugarcoat something brought his ire. Once in a while Ersty would speak up in a meeting with a funny comment followed by a sly grin that really caught you by surprise.

Later in our careers injuries took their toll on both of us, and we spent plenty of time together in the trainer's room. I might not have had lunches with him to cement our friendship, but I always knew he would be on the table beside me after the game. Groaning under the weight of our ice bags, we'd rehash all our frustrations, asking ourselves, "Why can't the game come as easily to us as it does to some of the others?" We were referring mainly to our hitting and the amount of mental effort it took to keep up with our ever-changing stances and mechanics. It might have looked easy to the fans, but we knew our weaknesses and had to work hard to conceal them. Ersty had a double whammy to boot. He also had to learn to play first base and the intricacies that came with it. But I've never seen anybody who worked harder than Ersty. He was always willing to do whatever it took to be successful. Even if that meant showing up seven hours before game time.

* * *

You might wonder why I have grouped Darin Erstad and David Eckstein together. In my mind, they are so much alike it was easier to just talk about them both at the same time. Actually, you could just about insert Eck's name into most of the descriptions I used for Ersty. The biggest difference between the two is the response you might get if you interrupted their routine. Ersty might bite your head off, where Eck would apologize profusely and excuse himself. You see, Eck is just too nice of a guy to ever be rude or mean. Truly a fan favorite, Eck will bend over backward to accommodate just about any request. People call me a straight-arrow, but as far as I'm concerned, when it came to having a totally aboveboard personal and professional life nobody surpasses David Eckstein. A man of tremendous character, Eck is as good as they come.

I remember the first time I saw Eck. I'm sure my initial thought wasn't much different than anyone else's upon first meeting. There I was in a big-league clubhouse with all these veritable physical specimens walking around. And then there was David. I am just glad that I didn't throw him my dirty uniform like I would have to any of the clubhouse attendants wandering around, because that's what he struck me as. Every bit of his 5'8" and 170 pounds made you think he couldn't possibly be a professional baseball player. His blond hair and youthful looks made him easily mistakable as someone's kid brother. But, there he was donning the same uniform as the rest of us, and covering a heart that had to be twice the size of anyone else's.

One of the things I love about Eck is his set of quirky rituals. Like a kid brother, I'd tease him and call them "superstitions" because it always got a rise out of him. "They're routines!" he'd exclaim. From the whirlybird bat warm-up to his first-step stealing technique that he practiced outside the dugout at game time, Eck was a treat to watch.

He did have some off-the-field routines as well. Unlike Ersty, Eck would go out to lunch with me, and over time, I got to know his eating routine pretty well. A huge fan of macaroni, just plain, he tried to eat it every day. And the pancakes made just right in the morning were a must, too. When we went on road trips, we were always challenging his eating "routines." When we ate at a restaurant, he would order the blandest thing on the menu and then ask if they could do something special to make it more bland. "Eck, you're in the big leagues now," we'd tell him. "Live it up a little!" But he'd stick to his guns and never show much variation.

As our leadoff hitter, Eck set the right tone for the game. I remember hearing once that Pete Rose, facing a pitcher he hadn't seen before, would tell his teammates, "You guys watch my first at-bat and you'll see every pitch this guy's got." That's how it was with Eck. Batting against any pitcher, he would take pitches and foul off balls until we saw the guy's entire repertoire. It was awesome. Eck would wear pitchers out before we ever got up there. Understanding that walks were just as good as hits, you could count on Eck taking a pitcher to a full count the majority the time. He would sprint down to first on a walk, always ready to display the hustle that set him apart from the pack. Having two hitters like Eck and Ersty ahead of me created plenty of hitting situations with men on base.

David Eckstein is a hero to lots of fans out there. His rise to success is a story they make movies about. He is the modern-day version of *Rudy* in so many ways. Always overlooked by bigger and more talented players, he is the guy who just keeps on plugging away, waiting for any opportunity to shine. When he finally does get his chance, there is not a more humble or gracious athlete out there. Always quick to give credit to God or his parents, sometimes even I wondered if he was too good to be true. Take my word for it: he is the real deal. He is as genuine as they come. His example of humility and the way he treats people are lessons we all can learn from. I have found myself on more than one occasion looking up (though not literally) to his example of great character and comparing my actions to his. He is one of the superstars of the game, and I am proud to say that my kids look up to him.

On the Down Slope

As I entered my early thirties, all the wear and tear I had accumulated through the years started to take its toll on my body. By 2001, trainers Ned Bergert and Rick Smith exhausted every resource available to them to keep me on the field. It was time for Dr. Yocum to wield his scalpel. He discovered that I had a frayed rotator cuff and some minor tears in my left shoulder. All the years of check swings had finally caught up to me. A cleanup is all that he could do at the time, and he felt confident I would be ready to play. After an intense rehab program, I learned that I would have to maintain a shoulder-maintenance program for the rest of my career. I was fortunate this time around, but the next time, my shoulder would need a complete overhaul.

Because my off-season consisted of mostly rehab rather than my typical strength-building training regime, I went into the season physically unprepared for the rigors of a full season. At the same time, I got on a cardio kick, which included a funky dieting regime to go along with it. I wanted to lose some weight, but looking back, 20 pounds was a little too excessive. I came in at about 220, about 15 pounds under my typical weight of 235. As the season progressed, the strain of games had me down to a weight I hadn't been in years.

One of the main reasons for surgery and my new health-conscious approach was that I was going into a contract year. Realizing that it probably would be my last multiyear contract, I was highly motivated to get healthy and be in the best shape possible when I became a free agent at the end of the season. When the Angels began discussing a contract extension with me, it was all contingent on me proving I was healthy in spring training. So a time frame was set in my mind. I had to prove my health, whether my body was ready or not.

Unfortunately, what started out as a physical issue quickly turned into a mental one. While my shoulder didn't necessarily hurt anymore, it clearly was not ready to be taking full swings at 90-plus miles per hour fastballs night after night. Very much in denial, I pushed through the slow start, convincing myself that I was always a slow starter and things would turn around. But sitting on a .200 average two months into the season with limited run production really started to chip away at my confidence. The season became a nightmare fast, and my mental ability to deal with it really took a toll on me. I found myself totally consumed with my failure 24 hours a day. I couldn't sleep for more than a couple hours at a time without waking up in a cold sweat, replaying my at-bats. I started to spiral out of control.

It was evident that I needed some help from the team doctors. After a couple of evaluations from outside physicians it was determined I was suffering from what they liken to "combat fatigue." I was in a cycle of no sleep and this was causing me to lose my focus during the games, which led to poor production and in turn, another night of no sleep. All the while, my body wasn't getting replenished, so I had no energy or strength to play the game. In my mind, I had fallen incredibly far, seemingly overnight. How could that be? I had always persevered through the tough times and always found a way out. Now, everything I tried came up empty. I might have had a nervous breakdown if it hadn't been for my faith and my family.

The Angels decided to put me on rest for two weeks based on the advice of the doctors. Sitting in Sosh's office and having Bill Stoneman break the news to me was a tough pill to swallow. It felt like I was admitting I was a failure and couldn't handle it anymore. It pains me to even type these words all these years later—that's how much it bothered me. But, something had to give, and it was the right move to make.

Playing the game when you are completely healthy is hard enough. Trying to do it when you are injured, the deck is really stacked against you. I guess I am writing about this because every player needs to know the limits of his own body, when he can play through injuries and the times when he can't. I thought I did. I had so much to prove going into that season from a contract standpoint that I lost all sense of perspective. I fooled myself into thinking I was healthy enough to start the season. To start just a month later might have made all the difference. But, unfortunately, as athletes we are hard-wired to fight through our struggles and live up to our responsibilities on the field. You see it happen all the time these days. A player comes back faster than he should and on most occasions struggles to regain the form everyone expects of him.

I came back after two weeks to play the rest of the 2001 season, and in 137 games I hit a dismal .227 with 17 homers and 49 RBIs. It was such a relief to finally have the nightmare season over. After a month at home to recharge and clear my head, I was motivated to start my off-season program again. Resuming a normal workout regime, I came into spring training in great shape and excited about the 2002 season.

The Bible verse James 1:2–3 reads, "Consider it pure joy, my brothers, whenever you face trials of many kinds, because you know that the testing of your faith develops perseverance. Perseverance must finish its work, so you may be mature and complete." It is this kind of divine wisdom that helps me get through the tough times in my life. I believe the trials one goes through are for a reason. I believed that the character I developed in 2001 must have been for a greater purpose. I was sure the coming year would be better. I just never dreamed it would be as great as it was.

When 2002 began on a similar sour note, the doubts that plagued my previous year slowly crept into my consciousness. After a particularly dismal April, I began to hear the whispers of those critics saying, "Maybe he's all washed up." As the stress mounted, I began to wonder it myself. Maybe the surgery on my shoulder would never allow me to get back to my normal caliber of play. The critics piled on, and it seemed like everyone from talk-show hosts, fans, and writers all got on the Tim Salmon retirement bandwagon.

Then, praise the Lord, my bat suddenly started to show some signs of life. In one particular game, I came off the bench to hit a late-inning game-tying home run off Toronto's Kelvim Escobar, and that seemed to be the hit that turned things around for me. I went on to hit .307 that May with a .411 on-base percentage. From that point on, I never looked back. I was in a groove that carried me all the way to August, when I was hit in the hand and missed most of the month. But I managed to get back on track again and finished the year with a .286 batting average, 22 homers, and 88 RBIs. My dramatic comeback earned me the *Sporting News* Comeback Player of the Year honors, but that was nothing compared to what our team got to experience that postseason.

After a terrible start, the team started improving around the middle of May. Late-inning heroics became our specialty, behind the Scioscia mantra of one inning at a time. We battled our way to a 99–63 record, four games behind the division-winning Oakland A's but enough for the wild card and our first playoff berth in 16 years. I entered October as the longest tenured player in the game without experiencing playoff baseball: 10 years and 1,388 games. Believe me, I was ready.

chapter 8

World Series Journal

Team Effort

When you experience a world championship, there's always going to be something special about the guys who accomplish it. A World Series–caliber team isn't one of those teams with 10 key players and the other 15 along for the ride. On a championship team, 25, maybe 28 guys play a part in it. That's how it was on our 2002 club.

From guys on the bench like Shawn Wooten, Benji Gil, and Orlando Palmeiro, to Brendan Donnelly and Scott Schoeneweis in the bullpen, every player on that roster had a dramatic impact on the team's success. To this day, I look at my team picture and have fun remembering each guy and his contributions. I can go right down the line that way. It was never about just one superstar carrying us the whole way. Every player had his time in the limelight. Adam Kennedy shined like you couldn't imagine in the ALCS, hitting three home runs in the series-clinching game. In the World Series, it was Garret Anderson's bases-clearing double that put us ahead in Game 7, despite being quiet throughout the postseason. Scott Spiezio and Troy Glaus had their turns in Game 6. My big moment came in Game 2. The bullpen featured the best arms in the game night after night, and Percy brought it home. And I'll never forget the amazing contributions of a couple of young phenoms, John Lackey and

Frankie Rodriquez. We learned how to rely on each other throughout the season, never putting too much pressure on a single person. This style of play made a difference in our postseason run.

The seeds of our success were sown eight months earlier back in spring training. We knew we had good pitching that could go toe to toe with anyone. What we needed was an offensive strategy, a way to manufacture runs from the tough pitching we would face in our division. Early on, we had a hitters' meeting. We knew we had a solid team, but we needed to find a way around the Oakland A's and their three-headed pitching monster—Tim Hudson, Mark Mulder, and Barry Zito. We decided that the best way to get to them was to scratch and claw any way we could to get three runs per game. So three became the magic number. We knew that if we could do that, we had the pitching to win those games. What it meant is that we had to take advantage of offensive situations differently than we had done in the past. If the situation called to move a runner over, then the hitter had to go the other way or bunt, just get the job done. There was no place for selfish players seeking individual glory or chasing statistics. Defining the mission was the easy part. Getting everyone to buy into it was the challenge.

I think we had just the right mix of guys on that club. Since the bulk of the players were "blue collar" guys, they responded to the new philosophy. Having guys like Ersty and Eck showing the way, we developed a style of play that would define our club. It was very clear, and everyone followed suit. With that mind-set in place, we really came together offensively. We worked on manufacturing runs, and as the season progressed, we gradually started building momentum. Playing really good ball, we found ourselves in a three-team race. Along with Seattle, we chased Oakland to the finish line. The A's captured the division, but we beat out Seattle and took the American League wild card.

I'll never forget arriving home after we clinched the wild card, playing in Texas. We landed in Orange County and boarded the buses to take us back to the ballpark. Then somebody noticed helicopters flying overhead. The bus was equipped with TVs, and the shout rang out, "Hey, we're on TV!" Our homecoming was being broadcast live on all of the local channels. When we got to the stadium, the parking lot was jam-packed with fans. It was an amazing feeling, especially after all those years of trying to get there.

Off we go to New York for the ALDS. Photo courtesy of AP Images

Wild Card

I have a theory about the postseason, and the last few years have really confirmed it. In 2002, the teams that had already clinched playoff spots were resting up, whereas we had to fight until the very last moment of the regular season to win the wild card. The teams that were coasting had to wait two weeks before turning the switch back on; our switch was never turned off. In our minds, the hard part was over. We had made it. It was the start of a new season—the postseason—and we were coming off an amazing high. We had a few jitters going in, as expected, but it wasn't anything different than what we'd been through in the last 30 games. As soon as we started playing the games, we felt right at home in the pressure-packed atmosphere.

We came in to the ALDS series against the Yankees as the underdog. I think that worked to our advantage as well. One might argue that New York had everything to lose and that we were in a win-win situation. That team is expected to win the World Series every year; we were practically written off before the season started. I'll never forget what hitting coach Mickey Hatcher said during our hitters' meeting at Yankee Stadium before the first game: "For most of you guys, it's the first time you've ever been here. All I can say is, just have fun and let it go. You may seem like the underdogs, but in 1988 when I was with the Dodgers, we were in the exact same situation. Back then no one gave us a chance to win, and you're the same kind of team. So believe me, you guys can do it. Just go out there and play."

There's not a better place on earth to experience the playoff fever than New York. Out on the streets Yankees fans went crazy when they saw us. We were the enemy, and the fans made sure we knew it. But that didn't bother us. Even after we lost Game 1 8–5, we kept our composure and fought back in Game 2 to beat the Yanks 8–6. We returned to Anaheim in a position to clinch the five-game series at home. Nobody particularly liked the idea of having to go back to the

Bronx and face Roger Clemens for Game 5. So we had to sweep our series at home.

They played tough in Game 3 and got out to an early lead, but we answered them with some hot hitting of our own. We roughed up Mike Mussina in the early innings so he gave way to the bullpen early on, but the Yankees held the lead through the game. Deadlocked at six after the seventh inning, I hit a two-run homer in the eighth off Steve Karsay to overtake the lead. Our bullpen was fabulous at holding a lead, and they did just that. Having the new addition in Frankie Rodriquez to set up for Percy really shortened the game.

I have always felt that the greatest pressure on the Yanks comes from the media and their great expectations. After we came back to win Game 3, you could just sense that the Yankees players knew the sharks were circling, waiting for blood. The truth is that we didn't have any doubts about winning. We had the right mojo going, and the Yankees didn't—it was evident in their body language. In the next game, we came out smoking with eight runs on eight hits in the fifth inning. Yankees outfielder Alfonso Soriano made a couple of key blunders that helped our cause, and just like that it was over. We beat them handily, 9–5, to move ahead to the ALCS. We probably made it look easier than it was, but our play was so impressive that at that point we started thinking *destiny*, the most fitting description of that magical month of October.

"Take It to 'Em Next Series!"

For the Angels organization, the next round was completely uncharted territory. Prior to beating the Yankees, the Angels had never won a playoff series. The Angels teams of the '70s and '80s had come close but had always fallen short. Now we had won our first series, and we were hungry for more. But first we needed to wait for the

Oakland–Minnesota series to wrap up. Publicly we said it didn't matter who won, but inside of the clubhouse I think we all wanted Minnesota. The A's were a very good team and they were deep in pitching, as we knew all to well. Their "three horses" could get hot at any moment and make it a very short series. The Twins, on the other hand, were much like us: a solid team that relied on everyone to get the job done.

Then again, beating the Minnesota Twins for the American League title was still a tall order. They played the same selfless, aggressive style of ball as we did—and they had a solid pitching staff. You could count on them coming at you hard for all nine innings. It was almost like looking at our own mirror image.

We got our wish: the Twins beat Oakland, so we were off to Minnesota. Unlike New York, there were no police escorts or angry hordes of fans waiting for us upon our arrival in the Twin Cities. With such little media and pregame fanfare it felt more like a regular season match-up than the American League Championship Series. On Media Day, we went into a little press area that had about one-fourth of the reporters we had encountered in New York. I recall walking in there and thinking, *Isn't the media coverage supposed to build each week in the playoffs?*

The Minnesota series was very much like the one we had just emerged from. Different series, but the same result. We lost the first game to the Twins, and then swept the remaining games. The key game was getting to Minnesota pitcher Brad Radke when we were at home. He had been our nemesis over the years. I'll admit it, he pretty much owned us. But when it really counted, we finally found a way to beat him.

In the series against New York, the big hits came from Glaus, Anderson, and me. Now against the Twins it was the two Benjis—Molina and Gil—Scott Spiezio, Brad Fullmer, and Adam Kennedy who stepped up big time. As it turned out in that series, our more

Unbelievable! Adam Kennedy's three homers in Game 5 of the ALCS helped propel us to our first pennant.

established players (me included) had problems with the Twins' pitching. It was the scrappers who picked us up during that whole series. My own bat stayed cool until the last game, when I went 3-for-4.

After the Twins beat us 2–1 in the opening game, Ersty and Fullmer powered us to a win in Game 2. Game 3 in Anaheim was a low-scoring squeaker. G.A. and Troy did most of the damage for us, each hitting solo homers. Pitcher Jarrod Washburn allowed the Twins only one run over seven innings, and Frankie and Percy finished it out in spectacular fashion.

Rookie John Lackey was brilliant on the mound in Game 4, and suddenly we were up 3–1 and only one victory away from our first pennant. We felt like a team of destiny, and others saw it, too. And then a funny thing happened before Game 5 that confirmed it for me. We had no regular batting practice scheduled on the field. Continuing the routine of hitting in the cages inside the stadium, I followed my usual routine: arriving early to the park, stretching, and then heading to the field for some loosening up under the sun.

I was out on the field stretching when some of the Twins wandered over to say hello. There was the usual small talk. Then as they turned to leave, one of the players turned back and told me, "You guys take it to 'em in the next series!" Suffice it to say, I was a little surprised at what I heard. He had just revealed to me that others could sense there was something special about our team. Players are the first to recognize inexorable momentum swings, and the Twins player was just stating the obvious. As a professional athlete, there are many times when you take the field against an opponent and get the sense they can do no wrong. That seemed to be the impression we were leaving on everyone.

When Game 5 started, there was a sense of urgency to win it and not let the series get back to Minnesota. The game belonged to Adam Kennedy, whose three consecutive home runs tied a postseason record shared by Babe Ruth and Reggie Jackson. Who would have guessed, before that series started, that A.K.'s nondescript Rawlings bat would end up being shipped to the Hall of Fame in Cooperstown?

It was amazing to see him hit his first two homers. He was very matter-of-fact about it. His third homer, though, was a shock because it wasn't supposed to happen. With two on in the seventh inning, Sosh gave Adam the bunt sign. After hitting two home runs, you would think he would be allowed to swing away, but that is not the way we did things that year. He bunted the first pitch foul and then fouled off another one swinging away. Down two strikes, he got a hanging curve from Twins reliever Johan Santana and smacked it over the wall in right center.

It was one of the most impressive performances I ever saw. Coming into the game 1-for-10 at the plate, A.K. saved the hits for when we needed them most. We won the game 13–5, and sitting in the locker room afterward in my champagne-soaked jersey I couldn't imagine anything better.

At my home in Phoenix I have a special baseball room with memorabilia and photos from my career. On the walls are panoramic shots of the numerous victory celebrations we had during that magical October in 2002. One of the photos was taken the moment we clinched the pennant against the Twins. What makes the shot really striking is the light and the way the shadows are falling on the field. I bring it up because it's exactly the way I still picture it in my mind. The picture perfectly evokes the special atmosphere that comes only in October. Playing baseball in the fall, the sun fades a little earlier and the cooler temperatures create a thickness in the air. When I look

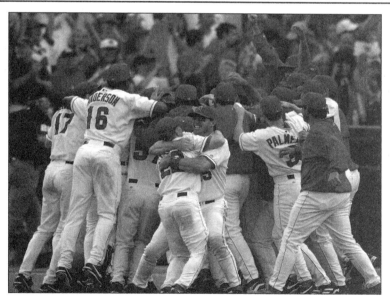

The autumn colors at the Big A made beating the Twins for our first pennant all the more surreal. Photo courtesy of AP Images

at that photograph, I feel that distinct sense of destiny that we had as a team during that October. We were rolling along, and everything was clicking perfectly. It was on to baseball's grandest stage, and the question on everyone's mind was, *Would our October magic continue?*

The Whole World Is Watching

Every kid growing up playing baseball has dreamed of playing in the World Series, and I was no different. My memories take me back to the mid-'70s, watching the Dodgers and Yankees go at it in the Fall Classic. A big fan of the Dodgers, I always imagined myself as Steve Garvey, the stoic leader of the team. Playing Pop Warner football at that time of year, the World Series was on everyone's mind and not football. Parents would be huddled on the sideline of our practices watching baseball on a little black-and-white TV. Those were good times growing up in Long Beach and riding the Dodgers' wave of success.

There I was 25 years later realizing my childhood dream, only doing it with the crosstown team I never followed as a kid. The anxiety and excitement was through the roof; the town was painted red! Everywhere you looked, you saw Angels banners and flags. Thinking back to 1992, when I first got called up, I never would have imagined the outpouring of fan enthusiasm that the World Series brought. It was a team mired in 35 years of bum luck. And now, a team that everyone had written off a month into the season was on the brink of making history. I could hardly sleep at night. It was really happening.

It is an indescribable feeling, playing a game when the eyes of the world are watching. The sobering realization is both exciting and terrifying. If you play well, you're the hero; if you play badly, you're the goat. Which would I be? What team was going to hold up under the bright lights and attention? I was hoping our red-hot team showed up to the World Series. We had been firing on all cylinders for the past two weeks, but time in between series might be enough to lose momentum. All we could do was trust in the routine Sosh set up for us and trust in each other.

There was some time to bask in the glory of the moment as well. Everyone had a story that the world was so interested in hearing. The most notable was our Energizer bunny, David Eckstein. His story seemed to capture the heart of anyone who was ever told they were too small. Scott Spiezio and I were goofing off with him by the on-deck circle during one of our workouts when a photographer asked us to pose with him. So we both grabbed Eck and held him sideways like we were carrying a log. As the camera clicked, we didn't realize until later that *People* magazine was doing a story on him and

Speez and I clown with Eck before the ALCS. Photo courtesy of AP Images

that picture would be featured. My wife was so pleased to see her hubby in her favorite magazine.

The World Series also brought a little bit of early Christmas to the guys in the clubhouse. All the equipment reps like Rawlings, Louisville Slugger, Nike, and Mizuno handed out their latest and greatest apparel and equipment.

In the midst of all the hoopla, it was imperative that we keep our edge. There was a series to play, and the guys in the San Francisco Giants' locker room wanted to win as much as we did. One of them was none other than future Hall of Famer Barry Bonds. As great a story as the Angels were, the World Series was for Bonds to put an exclamation point on his own career. All the MVPs are great players, but going to the Hall as World Series MVP was something even more special.

Barry was the big story coming out of the other clubhouse, and the world wanted to know how we were going to stop him. Without a doubt, it was a fine line to walk for Sosh and the pitchers trying to answer that. Would we pitch to him or not? We knew he was going to get his hits. We just hoped we could control the situation enough that it didn't hurt us. It was also interesting how the matchup was portrayed in the media. San Francisco was Goliath and the Angels David. Actually, *Bonds* was Goliath to our David.

To this day, I still wonder how the rest of the Giants players felt about the attention going solely to him. After all, it's not as if he got them there all by himself. Baseball is still a team sport, and the Giants had a few good ones of their own. One story close to my heart was that of J.T. Snow. He had come back home to exact revenge on the team that let him go so many years before. We were rookies together in 1993, and he was a great teammate and friend who we were all sad to see traded. After all those years apart, only one of us would be walking away with the prize. I was praying it would be me.

Opening Ceremonies

The day of the big game finally came. I was so anxious that I couldn't stand it. I must have checked the clock every 10 minutes, waiting to leave for the stadium. After what seemed an eternity of waiting around, I decided to leave early. I lingered around more in the locker room, but at least I was with the guys. Being able to get dressed and swing a bat a little alleviated some of my nerves. Taking the field for batting practice was an adrenaline rush, and seeing the sea of red filling the stands really got my juices flowing.

Opening ceremonies are always special in the playoffs, but the World Series takes it to a new level. After 30-something years, Angels fans finally got their World Series. After player introductions started, my emotions were off the chart. I have to admit, lining up along the third-base line in Angel Stadium was an especially proud moment for me and a couple of my teammates. Those prophetic words preached by Joe Maddon way back in the early days of Instructional League were finally coming true. There were only a few of us from that original class carrying the torch, but Percy, G.A., and I knew the historic implications for the organization better than anybody. The 2002 Angels were a team of destiny. Somehow we would come away victors.

Game 1 Jitters

Taking the field for the first pitch, I felt a rush that almost made me pass out. There is no way to simulate the level of excitement that surges through your body at a moment like that. Fortunately, I regained my composure and was able to settle down—a little bit. In a game where emotions are running high, you just can't wait to get that first at-bat and finally settle down. Standing in the outfield during that first inning, I'm lucky I didn't screw anything up because all that was on my mind was my first at-bat.

There are very few occasions I can ever remember my knees shaking while standing in the batter's box. This was one of them. But it all passed after the first pitch was thrown. Fouling off Jason Schmidt's first 97-miles-per-hour fastball, which looked more like a dart, caused a whole new set of concerns for a hitter. I'm thinking, *Was it the effect of the layoff between series? Did I jump at the ball? Or is he really throwing that hard?* It was probably a combination of all three factors, but I knew from the first pitch that he was going to be tough on us—and he was. I fouled off strike two and then swung at a fastball up in the zone to strike out.

In my second at-bat I fared a little better. I at least put the ball into play. (Unfortunately, a fly ball to center doesn't get the runner in from third base with two outs.) In the fifth inning after Eckstein's infield hit, Ersty followed with a single up the middle, putting runners on first and third with one out. Down 2–1 in the fifth inning we had a golden opportunity to put some runs on the board. Taking an aggressive approach, I swung at the first fastball and popped it up behind home plate. I hoped it might drift into the stands, but it stayed in play just enough for J.T. Snow to get under it. He initially slipped, but regained his bearings to make a spectacular catch. Schmidt then struck out G.A. to end the inning and our best threat of the game. I was now 0-for-2 with runners on third base—not exactly the heroics I dreamed about as a kid.

We went on to lose the first game of the series. But then again, what was new about that? We had lost Game 1 of the previous two playoff series and rebounded to win both series. It was time to turn the page and worry about Game 2.

Game 2: "Off the Hook"

The 2002 World Series followed the same script as the ALDS and ALCS. We had come up short in Game 1, losing a squeaker 4–3.

And we responded with a win in Game 2. The prevailing view on the team was *been there, done that.* There was no reason to panic. To drive our point home, we came out swinging the sticks like we had in the previous playoff series. The headlines in the *Orange County Register* read, "Off the Hook." It was a clever play on my name and the fact that I stepped it up after my poor performance in Game 1.

Game 2 was really a fun game to be a part of…as a hitter. In what turned into an offensive battle, both teams combined for 28 hits and 21 runs. The lead went back and forth as both teams battled it out like a great heavyweight title fight. The series really turned on this game. Hitters on both teams flushed out any anxieties they had and settled into offensive juggernauts. Fortunately, this was also true for me. After feeling like the goat the night before, a few hits, including a second-inning homer, bolstered my confidence once again, putting me in the right frame of mind for the biggest at-bat of my life. With the score tied 9–9 in the bottom of the eighth inning, the table was set for the first of many Angels heroics that would define the series for us.

With Felix Rodriguez on the mound, Adam Kennedy led off the inning by flying out to Lofton. Eckstein followed with a single, bringing the crowd to their feet. While Darin Erstad was at the plate trying to move Eck into scoring position, I was on deck doing my best to time Felix Rodriguez's fastball. The only positive for me in Game 1 was that I had a pretty good at-bat against Felix the night before. I finished that night on a pretty good swing and that was on my mind as I waited for my at-bat.

Having the opportunity to watch his fastball took away any apprehension I might have had at bat. He threw a hard fastball, but his three-quarter delivery got behind the ball in just a way that gave me a good look at it when it came into the hitting zone. As I stood in the on-deck circle, my mind was locked in on that slot, visualizing that pitch.

A side note to the 2002 season was that I had adjusted to hard-throwing pitchers. For the first time in my career, they didn't bother me anymore. After injuring my shoulder the previous year I started experimenting with different batting stances and discovered that by spreading my base out, it limited movement in my lower half, allowing me to spin on just about anything. Using my quick hands, it seemed I could just flick my hands at the ball. Down the stretch, I had hit a few home runs off hard throwers in key late-inning situations by doing just that. Now I actually looked forward to facing flame-throwers like Felix Rodriguez.

I also used a different bat for those late-inning pitchers. And no, it wasn't corked! Former coach George Hendrick turned me on to the bat he used in his day. It was a little M253 Louisville Slugger, measuring 33 inches long and 31 ounces. One inch shorter and smaller by a whole ounce than my regular stick, it is also much skinnier than most bats used today. It had a great feel to it, almost like a coach's fungo. It was light and hard as rebar, perfect against a guy like Rodriguez. Its lighter weight allowed me to wait a second longer on the pitch and still get around on the ball.

It was with this mind-set that I walked into the batter's box in the eighth inning of Game 2. With the game in the balance and with Eck on first base, I figured there was a good chance I'd get a fastball early in the count so that he'd get ahead of me with a strike. Always the threat to steal a base, Felix needed to keep an eye on Eck, which further enhanced my chances of getting a good pitch to hit early in the count. Sure enough, the first pitch Rodriguez gave me was a heater out over the plate, and I squared it up perfectly. As soon as I hit it, I knew it was gone. Suddenly we were up 11–9.

What player hasn't dreamed of hitting a big home run in the World Series? Usually I'm not one to show up an opposing pitcher by jogging slowly around the bases. This time though, I had to make an exception. Rounding first, I deliberately slowed my pace to savor the moment. I remember, back in the mid-1990s, hitting plenty of home runs when the stadium was half full. Never in my wildest dreams could I have imagined it would be as sweet as this one. Was I dreaming? Rounding third, I gave a fist pump to coach Ron Roenicke and realized it was for real. As I made my way to the plate I saw Eck standing off to the side, totally pumped. As I trotted to the mosh pit in the dugout, the whole team was jubilant.

Years of wondering if I had what it took to come through in a major clutch situation were vanquished forever with that one swing.

To say I was thrilled is an understatement. I finally proved to myself I could come through when it mattered most. Photo courtesy of AP Images

To experience that elation with my teammates, to come through for them when it really counted, was a tremendous release. Years of pent-up emotion came pouring out of me like water through a broken dam. After the game I was all smiles and laughter, and guys were saying, "Who is this? We haven't seen this kind of emotion from him his whole career!"

My home run doesn't compare to the drama-filled, spectacular home run Kirk Gibson hit for the Dodgers back in 1988, but it was just as crucial for our team and for me. It proved to be a game-winner, and the victory gave us the momentum boost we needed as we headed up to San Francisco.

Bonds' Blast

It amazes me what sticks in people's memories about the World Series. One of the first things people always ask me about is Barry Bonds' home run in Game 2. Of all the highlights during that series, people still remember my reaction from the dugout railing because of the media play Fox TV gave it. Of course, I had no idea I was even on camera, but my reaction helped underscore the storyline that Barry Bonds was truly amazing.

After taking a two-run lead in the bottom of the eighth inning and retiring the first two batters, the stage was set for power against power: Troy Percival, hardest thrower in the game versus Barry Bonds, the "home run king." It was the matchup everybody was anxious to see. Would Percy challenge him? I wasn't sure Sosh would let him with the game on the line, but in a situation where one run wouldn't hurt us, Percy was given the green light.

Percy's first pitch was 98 miles per hour up and a little outside. From the sidelines, it looked like pure heat and it seemed Percy might have the edge in this first meeting. Before you could comment on it,

Getting by the Giants meant getting by the great Barry Bonds, no easy task.

Percy kicked into his familiar high-leg windup, firing the next laser. The ball exploded off of Bonds' bat as if it had been shot from a cannon. To see something moving that fast change trajectory so quickly was truly awe-inspiring. From the dugout, I tracked the ball as it carried high and deep into the night air, way beyond the typical home-run graveyard. Then, like a ghost ball or an apparition, it vanished perfectly into one of the tunnels leading into the concession stands.

Like everyone else in the stadium, I was astonished. Leaning against the railing, I said to myself, "Oh, my gosh! I've never seen a ball hit that far!" It was only after the game that I found out that I wasn't talking to myself after all. About 20 million fans read my lips, because right after the blast the Fox TV cameras had cut to the Angels dugout for a reaction and caught me mouthing those now famous words.

Barry Bonds was an incredible hitter, and from my vantage point, that hit still is the longest home run I've ever seen. Indeed, the story-line made it all the more impressive. Percy still gives me a hard time (in jest, of course) about my public reaction and the fanfare it received. If it had been a game-winner, I probably wouldn't have shown such dumbfounded emotion from the dugout. But it wasn't a game-changer. And it was just as impressive that Percy stood up to the challenge of Bonds with his best stuff. There's got to be consolation in that, because a walk would have been worse.

Gut-Check Time

Up until then, we had been swinging the pole and having fun. It turned out that the pressure and intensity wasn't as intimidating as we thought it would be. We were playing the same kind of game we'd been playing for the last couple months. All we had to do was win two of the next three games in San Francisco, and we'd be coming back home in a great position.

So naturally, we *lost* two out of three. Instead of returning home conquering heroes we felt like we'd barely survived a fall off the Golden Gate Bridge. Faster than you could say "blow-out," the fun was over. After we got whacked 16–4 in the Frisco finale, the mood in the clubhouse was absolutely melancholy. It's one thing to lose when you're playing well, but to have everything unravel like it did in Game 5 was downright sobering.

I'll never forget how silent the bus ride to the airport and our flight back home were. Nobody said a word. It was as if we were heading for a funeral. It was almost 2:00 AM when the buses finally dropped us off at the stadium in Anaheim. Driving home with Marci was no less depressing when we passed by the Big A on the 57 freeway. We had become so accustomed to seeing the lights illuminating the Halo after a win, and now it was eerily dark, as if it were signifying that the season was over. It was a horrible notion that seemed to strike us both simultaneously. We blurted it out almost in unison: "I wonder if it would have been better to have never gotten this far than to come all this way and lose."

It was an eerie moment. We looked at one another in astonishment, and in that instant the World Series took on a whole different meaning for me. From that moment, everything I'd thought regarding the entire postseason experience was turned on its head.

For many of us, just getting to the Series was a once-in-a-lifetime experience, a huge reward in its own right. But now to finally be there and not finish the job was unbearable. We had gone from wild-card winners with nothing more expected of us and therefore nothing to lose, to the Series favorite with everything to lose.

With the stakes so high, we knew that Game 6 would be memorable. Little did we know it would be one for the ages and the defining moment of a franchise steeped in 41 years of bad luck and futility.

"Dude, We're Back in This"

In Game 6 the Giants ran starter Russ Ortiz out to the mound. We had hit him pretty hard in Game 2, and we felt pretty confident going into the game—maybe too confident. As the fifth inning rolled around, he had thrown a gem. We missed a golden opportunity in the sixth to score some runs when, with runners on second and third, I struck out looking to end the inning. It was one of those at-bats when you're so locked in on a certain zone and the pitcher completely surprises you with something else. I was sitting on something out over the plate when he threw me an inside cutter that just caught the inside corner. Walking back to the dugout, I was disgusted at the call. We were running out of chances to get back in the game.

Coming off the field in the seventh, I went directly downstairs to the video room to review my at-bat and the last pitch. I became even more despondent, because what I *just knew* had been a blown call now looked like a strike after all. And I was going to have to live with that strikeout for the rest of my life.

Trailing 5–0 in the seventh inning, it would have been easy for us to start reflecting on the Series-ending loss that seemed inevitable. Now I could imagine what the Twins and the Yankees felt as they saw everything going right for us. Then destiny stepped in. The momentum slowly swung in our favor, giving us one last chance. Consecutive hits by Glaus and Fullmer signaled the end for Russ Ortiz. Giants manager Dusty Baker went out to the mound to make a change. Baker gave him a pat on the back to signal a job well done. As a token of his "game-winning" performance, Baker slipped the game ball into the departing Ortiz's glove.

Much has been made of that incident since then, but I don't remember anyone on the bench even noticing it at the time. I guess I can see the argument against handing out a game ball before the game is over. Still, I don't remember it being a motivating factor to our comeback. Some might say it disrupted the karma or rattled the baseball gods, but I don't buy into that either. What happened from that moment on is more a reflection of the character of our team. If we would have known that a bottle of champagne was opened prematurely in the Giants' clubhouse—which it was—then that could have been a motivating factor.

As I reviewed my last strikeout, I kept an eye on the game monitor to watch Speez face Felix Rodriguez. Continuing his gritty hitting in that whole postseason, he was putting together an at-bat for the ages. Working it to a full count, he kept fouling off pitch after pitch until he got one he could handle. Then the unthinkable happened. On the eighth pitch of his at-bat, Rodriguez missed one down and inside, and Scott blasted a momentous three-run homer down the right-field line. It seemed an eternity for that ball to come down. I put it right up there with Roy Hobbs' dramatic home run in *The Natural.*

I can't believe what I just saw! I admit that phrase has been used before, but it was exactly what I was thinking. In a flash, I came sprinting up the stairs toward the dugout to celebrate. Bounding up the steps, I got there to greet Fullmer just as he screamed, "Dude, we're back in this!" He knew I was frustrated from my last at-bat, and what he was really saying was, "You just got another chance."

In the eighth, down 5–3, Ersty led off the inning, and hit a hanging changeup on the third pitch from Tim Worrell, depositing it into the right-field stands. Sensing another unbelievable comeback was on the brink, the crowd erupted into pandemonium. We had erased four runs in two innings, and were now only trailing by one run. *I could tie the ballgame up with one swing!* That was the thought in my mind as Ersty rounded the bases.

Luckily, I came to my senses and didn't lose focus. With no outs and no one on, we just needed a base runner, not a home run. If I could get on base, rookie speedster Chone Figgins would pinch-run for me. In the last month of the season Sosh had employed this strategy in my last at-bat, replacing my defense with Alex Ochoa's glove. Figgy proved to be a tremendous asset down the stretch because he could score so many different ways with his speed.

I approached the at-bat like I was leading off an inning, reminding myself that I just needed to get on base, so I needed to be patient and stay within myself. *Take what he gives me and don't expand the zone,* I thought to myself. I knew Worrell threw a hard cutter away. It's not a pitch most righties can turn on, so I eliminated the thought of getting the head of the bat out and trying hit a home run to left field. I focused instead on staying up the middle with the pitch.

The situation played out just as everyone hoped. Hitting a line drive to center on the second pitch, I got to first and didn't even have to wait for coach Alfredo Griffin to make it official. Sosh had Figgy on his way, representing the tying run, almost a lock with nobody out. My night was over. All that was left for me was to cheer on my teammates.

G.A. came up after me. He had been swinging a pretty quiet bat in the series, but we all knew he was a double-hitting machine, and one right now would tie the game easily. And wouldn't you know it, he finally got that much-needed hit. The theory behind getting out of a slump is to just bloop a hit anywhere; the emotional release is usually enough to get your confidence back. The timing couldn't have been better. G.A. blooped a lazy fly ball down the left-field line that allowed Figgy to motor around second base and into third. Figgins' aggressiveness forced Bonds to misplay it, allowing a hustling G.A. to slide into second. The Angels were in business.

Now with the tying and go-ahead runs in scoring position, the red-hot Troy Glaus headed to the plate. The Giants brought in their closer, Robb Nen, figuring it was their best chance to preserve the lead. Once again I hustled downstairs to watch the at-bat on the monitor and do some scouting. Even in a clutch moment like this, I still wanted to see the way Nen would attack Glaus. Nen seemed to be avoiding Troy with his slider. In a 2–1 count, he tried to throw the slider away and hung it over the heart of the plate. Troy stayed on the ball and roped it into deep left-center field. From my vantage point, it took a few anxious moments to realize it split the gap between Bonds and Lofton. As the ball carried over Bonds' head, I charged back up the stairs into the total bedlam of the Angels bench. We took the lead, and the stadium went crazy.

Troy's bases-clearing double completed one of the most improbable comebacks in World Series history. Just two innings prior, the Giants were preparing the postgame celebration in their locker room. Now, as Percy was jogging in to slam the door shut on their celebration, clubhouse attendants were scrambling to remove the victory champagne and plastic tarps that covered the lockers.

When I left the ballpark that night on the 57 freeway, I looked over at the Big A from the parking lot and saw the halo lit and shining brightly. Order seemed to return to the Angels' universe, restoring our hopes for the next day's Game 7. Thanks to the most unbelievable finish to a game as I've ever witnessed, the momentum was back on our side.

Chapel Sunday

David and Goliath

In the late '90s, when the Yankees were in their heyday, most people would have been surprised to learn how many Christian believers were on that team. Chad Curtis told me that 15 to 20 guys attended team chapels regularly. On the road, the biggest stars on that team would have Bible studies in their hotel rooms after the game. They met for a daily devotion and a prayer before taking the field as well. It was amazing to hear that such a great team was so reliant on God to meet its daily needs, aligning its perspectives with God's and careful not to get too caught up in its own success.

Our team, the 2002 Angels, were a very similar group of guys. We always had great turnouts for chapels and Bible studies on the road. God's hand was at work, doing amazing things in the lives of a lot of our players. And like most World Series Game 7s, this one fell on a Sunday, which meant we would have one last opportunity for chapel before the game. This was one chapel guys didn't miss.

Anatomy of a Win

Six Crucial Moments in Game 6

With one out in the bottom of the seventh, Dusty Baker gives starter Russ Ortiz the game ball.

Two batters later, Scott Spiezio hits a three-run home run.

Erstad's leadoff homer in the eighth makes it 5–4 Giants. Photo courtesy of AP Images

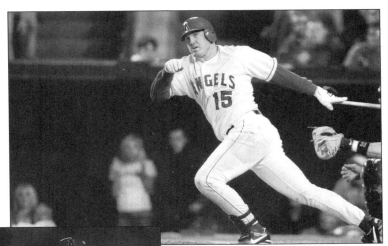

I follow with a single to center to keep things going.

Having Chone Figgins pinch-run for me was a smart move. His speed forces Bonds to misplay G.A.'s single and puts two runners in scoring position.

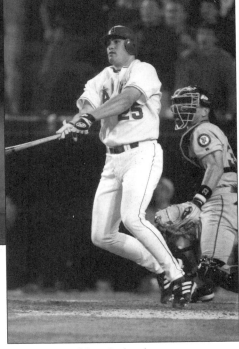

Troy Glaus' clutch two-run double seals the deal.

Chapel Sunday was a constant throughout my career. Before Game 7, pastor Chuck Obremski (to my immediate right) got everyone—including starting pitcher John Lackey—to loosen up.

Chuck Obremski was a local pastor and chaplain for the team. A chaplain for more than 15 years for the L.A. Rams before they left town, he had plenty of locker-room experience. Over the years he had developed a great rapport and deep friendships with the Angels players. We had plenty of trainers attending to our physical needs; Chuck saw to our spiritual, and sometimes emotional, needs. He encouraged us to keep perspective and reminded us that we could accomplish great things when we are aligned with God's will. Meeting in one of the auxiliary locker rooms, Garret, Speez, Eck, and I were talking with Pastor Chuck in our makeshift chapel when starting pitcher John Lackey ambled in. "What's new, John?" Chuck asked with a wink. With the weight of the world on his shoulders, Lackey could only muster a half-hearted grin. "Hey, man," Chuck said playfully, trying to lighten the mood, "It's not like you're pitching Game 7 of the World Series or anything." Then he added earnestly, "It's just a baseball game, so go ahead and have some fun."

Chuck liked to make wisecracks and jokes that drew him into the players' world of typical locker-room banter. His message for us that morning was taken from Samuel 1:17: the story of David and Goliath. David was the young Israelite boy who slew the nine-foot-tall Goliath with a mere slingshot. Displaying a confidence way beyond his youth, David did what the rest of the army was too terrified to do: stand up to the giant in the name of God and claim victory. The Angels were just like David, Chuck said, battling and slaying Goliaths all season long, against the tallest of odds. We had come out of nowhere to do amazing things, said Chuck, and more than anything else, we could all acknowledge it was by God's grace that we stood there that morning on the brink of greatness.

"There's not a prima donna in this room!" he exclaimed. "Every one of you, all year long, was willing to say, 'If it's in the best interest of the team, then I'm willing to do it.' If that meant bunting or hitting behind the runner, you did it. You were more concerned about winning as a team than attaining individual acknowledgement."

Amen to that! Our teamwork was exactly the reason why we were now just one victory away from baseball's ultimate prize. Now, just like David, we were being called upon to be brave and rely on God for the final outcome.

Chuck delivered to us just what we needed that last chapel Sunday. It was a message of inspiration for all those who were willing to trust in God when facing the giants in our lives. Each one of us carried a gut full of pressure and anxiety into that room, not the least of whom was rookie John Lackey, on whose arm we would rely that night. After

Chuck's message we bowed our heads, giving thanks to the God who makes all triumphs possible, and then loaded up our slingshots.

G.A.'s Our Man

It is a weird feeling to come to the ballpark knowing that today is the last game of the season. Tomorrow everyone goes home and the long season is officially over. *Will I be a world champion at the end of the night?* That question keeps running through my head. Parking my car in the players' lot I can't help but think, *The next time I get in my car, I will either be a world champion or extremely disappointed.*

We had every reason to feel good about our chances, though. The emotional high from Game 6 was a huge momentum change. Destiny seemed to be on our side. I was sure we would win the game that night. We had come too far that season to be denied. Then again, I'm sure the Giants shared the same sentiment.

Taking the field in a game for all the marbles, you could feel the tension in the air. We tried to stay loose by cracking a few jokes, but it was just a thin veil masking our anxieties. There was no getting around the fact that after 178 games, our year came down to this.

John Lackey, the 24-year-old rookie called up at the end of the season, took the hill. There was some talk within the media that we were asking too much from the kid. Sosh and the staff felt he was our best option and that he could handle it. A standout quarterback in high school, John played in some big games in Lubbock, Texas, but that was nothing compared to this stage. If he won tonight, he would be the first rookie in 93 years to win a Game 7 in the World Series. It was truly uncharted territory.

Livan Hernandez was the starter chosen by Dusty Baker. Already the recipient of a World Series ring with the Florida Marlins, he clearly had experience weighing in his favor. Still, we were relieved; the arm we were hoping not to see was Jason Schmidt's.

In the second inning, Lackey experienced his first test. The Giants had runners on the corners with one out. After a sacrifice fly by Reggie Sanders pushed one run across, Lackey settled down to get the final out. All in all, it was pretty good damage control by the rookie. We answered right back for him. Benji Molina drove in Speez with a double off the top of the wall in left-center field in the bottom half of the inning.

Heading into the bottom of the third inning, Eck got things started with a leadoff single. Then Ersty followed with a liner to left to give us runners on first and second with no outs. I came to the plate looking to keep the inning going. Working the count to 2–2, Livan threw the next pitch high and tight to get me off the plate. Like

If I had to choose one person to send to bat with the World Series on the line it would be G.A. There was never a doubt in my mind that he would not come through. Photo courtesy of AP Images

a heat-seeking missile, the ball chased me and hit me on my top hand, pinching the tip of my middle finger against the bat. I was pretty sure it was broken. Through my split batting glove I could see the finger swelling. After a few moments of discussion with our trainer Ned Bergert and Sosh, I stayed in the game. It was only the third inning, and there was no way I was coming out of the game unless I couldn't swing the bat.

As I stood on first base feeling an unmistakable sense of destiny pour over me, Ersty was on second, Eckstein was on third, and coming to the plate was arguably the best hitter the Angels ever had. *The stars are aligned perfectly,* I thought. If you could pick any hitter in Angels history to come to the plate with the bases loaded in Game 7 of the World Series, Garret Anderson would be the man. The best hitter to ever wear an Angel uniform, we had our man when we needed him most. But that wasn't all. Outside of Eckstein, every Angels on the field was a homegrown talent. We had it in our hands to accomplish everything the organization had set out to achieve.

G.A. lived up to his billing. With the count 1–1, he slammed a rocket right over my head and down the right-field line. As soon as he hit it I knew I was scoring. I'd hit in front of G.A. my whole career; I must have scored 100 times from first on hits just like this one. I ran the bases in an extra gear that hadn't existed in years. After crossing the plate and high-fiving Ersty and Eck, I looked back at second base to give G.A. a fist pump. In his typical fashion, he didn't break so much as a smile, but he gave himself a nonchalant little golf clap, as if to say that there wasn't much difference between the biggest hit of his life and an ordinary double he'd hit hundreds of times in his career. Still, I knew from that small reaction that he was excited inside. G.A., the Doubles-Hitting Machine, had done it again, clearing the bases.

Fans can say what they want about his lack of enthusiasm on the field, but it doesn't matter one bit to me. G.A. is a gamer. And in the biggest game in Angels history, with the world's attention focused on baseball's biggest stage, Garret slammed the clutch double that won us the World Series. I would have bet the farm on him in the situation. And when he clapped his hands, it was for Garret an overwhelming display of emotion—almost as momentous as the hit that occasioned it.

Lights Out

After scoring all the runs we would need for the game in the third inning, it was the pitching staff that took center stage in Game 7. Lackey got through five innings with the gutsiest performance you could imagine from a rookie in his situation. Passing the baton to our greatest asset, the bullpen, Game 7 played out according to our script. Brendan Donnelly came in to chew up the sixth and seventh innings, bridging the gap to get us to Frankie Rodriguez. Frankie continued his dominance, carving up the heart of the Giants order.

After striking out in the eighth inning, I was replaced with Alex Ochoa as a defensive move. The realization set in that with no Game 8 tomorrow, the series was over for me. For the first time in eight months, I had no further duties that would affect the outcome of the game or series. I was a spectator with nothing to do—and as nervous as a cat.

With a 4–1 lead and Percy coming in to pitch the ninth inning to lock down the win, the dugout bench was empty. Everyone was on the top step leaning on the rail. J.T. Snow capped off his great series with his third hit of the night, giving the Giants a leadoff single. Could the disgruntled player we traded away years ago become the fly in the ointment that ruined our celebration plans? I couldn't help but worry; this one was going to be a nail-biter to the finish.

Without Francisco Rodriguez, we wouldn't have won the Series. His presence was huge.

Then, out of the corner of my eye, I noticed Jackie Autry and her entourage coming up the tunnel to the dugout in preparation for the victory celebration. A wave of panic rushed over me. *Oh my gosh,* I thought. *I know they want to be a part of all this, but don't they know being on the bench right now might jinx things for us?*

Just the night before, the Giants seemed to be on their way to winning the Series, going into the seventh inning with a 5–0 lead. We ended up winning 6–5, and rumor had it that some Giants personnel, setting up the visiting clubhouse for celebration, had jinxed the Giants by breaking open a bottle of champagne before the game was over. It was a big no-no—if it was true.

I didn't know if Mrs. Autry was packing champagne, but her very presence in the dugout while the game was still being played might be enough to put the jinx on us all, so I decided to run some interference. Besides, if the Giants did tie the game, we would have to hustle Mrs. Autry and her entourage out of the dugout, and no way could that be handled lightly. After all, how do you tell the owner of the team that she isn't welcome in the dugout?

I don't think any players or coaches even noticed the impending invasion. With the rest of the team standing at the railing watching the game, I made a beeline for the bat rack, grabbed a bat and helmet, and started taking practice swings. I hoped that this would serve as a visual reminder of who should be there. To the players, it was still business as usual in the dugout. That was the message I was trying to get across. The organization already had a laundry list of curses and jinxes. I have the greatest respect for Mrs. Autry, but you can bet that, had we lost the game, and it was discovered that she was in the dugout, it would have been proclaimed forever that the Angels lost the World Series because Jackie Autry jinxed us. Fortunately, my ploy worked, and I was able to keep premature celebration at bay, and out of the dugout.

Tribal Fears

There is not a more pressure-packed time in a game than the ninth inning with the game in the balance. Many a pitcher has been thrown into that save situation only to realize he can't handle the heat. Having an experienced closer to come in and nail down the game is crucial, and the Angels had just that in Troy Percival. Relying on more than just a 95-miles-per-hour fastball, Troy has the mental toughness to battle through whatever crazy jam he might get into with the game on the line. Over the years he's had his share of close calls and failures, but he always gets back on the hump the next night to get the job done.

There was one team, though, that accounted for most of these fits: the Cleveland Indians. Back in the mid-'90s, they were the one team that always seemed to have his number. Tribe batters Jim Thome, Albert Belle, and Richie Sexson all hit game-winning hits or walk-off homers off Percy. As a group of hitters, they all seemed to have something on Troy, some kind of tip of the pitch that resulted in very confident swings on the other side. Suspicions were high because it seemed to be the only team in baseball that did this to Troy. So after giving up a leadoff single to J.T. Snow, Percy settled down and got the next guy out, walked one, and struck out the next batter. With two outs in the ninth, just one batter stood between us and the ultimate prize; his name was Kenny Lofton, a former Cleveland Indian.

To most pitchers, Lofton's name wouldn't evoke much fear, but those who knew him in the mid-'90s when he was the pesky leadoff hitter for the Tribe might understand my uneasiness as I watched from the bench. If Cleveland had something on Percy that gave them an advantage—say he was unconsciously tipping his pitches, for instance—then Lofton would certainly remember that and be ready. As hard as I tried to suppress my negative thoughts, they just wouldn't go away. *Does he still have a "book" on Percy?* Sometimes the most unlikely candidates to hit a home run are the very ones to do it.

Be very careful here, Percy, I thought to myself. *Lofton can hurt us, so please, just don't give him anything good to hit.* Lofton went after the first pitch and connected. Now, any time a hitter takes a full swing off a guy throwing 95 miles per hour, any upward trajectory can make your heart skip a beat. The ball flew out toward right-center field and I immediately looked to see Ersty's reaction. An outfielder's body language is usually a good indication of how well the ball was hit. Ersty tracked toward the wall at first, but when he began waving his arms, I knew he had it and started to breathe again. I pled under my breath, "Two hands, Ersty! Squeeze it! Don't let that ball come out of your glove."

When Lofton came to bat, I don't think anyone besides maybe Garrett, Ersty, and I gave any thought to Troy's troubling history against the Indians. Maybe it wouldn't even have occurred to me if I had still been in the game by then. But being on the bench made me a spectator like everyone else, analyzing every situation and its possibilities. Knowing our past failures, I knew well enough that Lofton was far from an automatic out.

After the pileup on the field, I found Jackie Autry, embraced her, and thanked her for everything she had endured over the years with her husband, Gene, in the service of this team. It was an awesome moment for us all. The Singing Cowboy finally got his championship.

Let the party begin. Photo courtesy of Getty Images

Patches, Hats, and History

Over the years I wore several commemorative patches on my game jerseys. Two of them were especially meaningful to me. One was in honor of our beloved coach Jimmie Reese, who died in 1994. The other patch honored Angels owner Gene Autry after his death in 1998.

In 2002, as we edged closer to a world championship, I wanted to do something special to commemorate the franchise and pay tribute to those who came before me. After sharing my desire with my good friend Tim Mead, a longtime front-office executive with the

The most beloved Angel, Jimmie Reese. To honor his memory, I kept a patch in my pocket throughout the World Series with his initials, as well as one with Mr. Autry's.

team, we came up with a few ideas. Because no two people represented the Angels tradition more than Jimmie Reese and Gene Autry,
I decided to carry their special patches in my pockets throughout the
postseason. They were both outstanding men who poured their lives
into this organization, and I was proud to be able to honor them in
this way.

As the longest-tenured player on the team, I was the link between
the old guard and the new. A lot of the younger guys didn't have an
appreciation for the long frustration that plagued our organization.
As the elder statesman, I felt a responsibility to bring it all together
for them and the fans. It was always Mr. Autry's dream to win a world
championship, and as we finally neared that goal, I wanted to be prepared, should we accomplish it. Carrying his patch in my pocket was
a personal thing, but given the opportunity, we needed to do something special as a team.

With the exception of Troy Percival, perhaps, no one in the clubhouse knew Jackie Autry, Gene's widow, better than I did. I told her
that I wanted to do something to celebrate and honor her husband if
we won the World Series. When she asked what I had in mind, I half-
seriously suggested that it might be a perfect tribute to the original
Singing Cowboy if all of the players rode around the stadium on
horseback wearing white Stetson cowboy hats.

Jackie appreciated the sentiment, but suggested that having 25
baseball players—some of whom had never been on a horse before—
rodeo riding around the ballfield in front of 45,000 screaming fans
might not be the best idea. So we nixed the horses and instead
decided that I would don her husband's favorite cowboy hat during
the victory celebration.

Jackie brought Gene's old Stetson to me the next day. It turned
out to be way too small for my head. So I figured I'd just pass it
around to the players during the celebration. After the final out, I

asked one of the clubhouse kids to go to my locker to retrieve it. After waving it around a few minutes, I looked to pass it along and gave it to David Eckstein. Not aware of my intentions, he just grabbed it and put it on. It fit him perfectly. I figured there was no player to honor the memory of Mr. Autry better than a player like Eck, so he wore it the rest of the night. So that's why you see him wearing that hat in all the celebration photos.

Victory Lap

In every sporting event, it seems as if the victors always parade the championship trophy around for the fans. During our division- and league-championship celebrations, I had the privilege of running those trophies around the field to share with the fans. The victory laps weren't preplanned, but being the veteran on the team, it seemed like the right thing to do at the moment.

After the World Series on-field celebration, I ran into the clubhouse and started in on the champagne. Mike Scioscia followed shortly thereafter holding the championship trophy he had just received on the field. As I approached him to get a better look at the trophy, he handed it to me and said, "Here, Fish. Go take this outside." Not one to argue with my manager, I beelined it back onto the field to share it with the players and the fans still celebrating in their seats.

Let me tell you, after playing seven intense games, a World Series trophy is very heavy. If I had known this ahead of time I might have come up with as alternative idea. A few of us started showing the trophy to the fans behind the dugouts. I figured I would carry it to the pitcher's mound or maybe first base, and that would be that. But the fans were on their feet cheering and clapping, and things just snowballed. Taking off down the first-base

Here I am, doing my best to stay ahead of the reporters and share the magic of the moment with the fans. Photo courtesy of Getty Images

line, I realized pretty quickly the few guys who were with me had fallen back. Now the parade consisted a bunch of photographers and me. I kept running, more media people kept joining in, and pretty soon I felt like the Pied Piper. A bunch of them got in front of me as I ran, and I remember thinking, *Oh my gosh, if one of these guys stumbles and takes me down, I'm going to plant this trophy like a lawn dart!* I had a terrifying picture in my mind of a mangled mess of metal with chunks of grass stuck to it. That would have looked nice in Mrs. Autry's display case.

I was so burdened by the cumbersome trophy and by my anxiety about dropping it, that by the time I got to the right-field foul pole I could hardly hold it up anymore. My shoulders burned and ached, and on top of that, I could feel the effects of the champagne kicking in. I was gasping, wondering how I was going to make it around the whole field. Looking around for someone to help, I saw only reporters, so I sucked it up and kept going. When I neared the third-base line I saw Scot Shields and Shawn Wooten. "Come over here!" I yelled. "Help me hold this!" They were happy to oblige, giving me a much-needed relief. To this day, the one photo that I often get asked to sign at card shows has me holding the trophy and includes Shields and Wooten in the foreground helping me. Shieldsy still laughs about it. "Fish," he says, "You don't know how many times people ask me to sign this thing."

Looking back on those memories, I could not have been prouder to take that victory lap. I felt a special connection with the fans, many of whom had waited 40 years for a world championship. I wanted to share that incredible moment with the people in the stands who deserved it as much, if not more so, than any of us, through their incredible loyalty and patience over the years. To share something like that with our fans was absolutely priceless.

Welcome to Hollywood

After winning the World Series, I had a recurring nightmare for months to follow. I kept dreaming that I had to play Game 7 again. I would wake up in a cold sweat and remind myself, *Yes, we did win the World Series.*

After celebrating all night with my family, some of us were asked to be back at the stadium at 1:00 the next afternoon.

Jay Leno, host of *The Tonight Show*, had requested that the nucleus of the team come on his show. So there we were, Percy, Eck, Speez, Lackey, and me, chauffeured to the NBC Studios in Burbank just like rock stars. I remember thinking that we'd really hit the big time. Back in the green room, Jay came in to introduce himself and prepped us about what he wanted to talk about on camera. When we

What better way to top off an unbelievable week than with a visit to The Tonight Show? Photo courtesy of AP Images

came out and sat on television's most famous couch, he started asking us the questions he'd prepped us for. It was all fun and exciting—until Jay tossed me a wicked curveball.

A researcher on *The Tonight Show* staff had found an article about me that contained this quote from my wife: "When Tim wasn't hitting or was in a slump, I'd always tell him to stick his butt out more in his stance." Jay read the quote, looked at me with a huge smile, and said, "What exactly are we talking about here, Tim? What does this stance look like? Why don't you stand up and demonstrate it?"

The studio audience started to cheer and clap in encouragement, and for a moment I just sat there kind of frozen. You've got to be kidding me! You want me to get up in front of the whole world and stick my butt out? I know it was part of my batting stance that the whole world saw in the game the night before, but for some reason this kind of exhibition of my backside didn't seem right. I would've liked to decline or just turn invisible, but I quickly realized that there was nothing to do but be a good sport and play along. So I got up and demonstrated my batting stance and gave the audience a little waggle for some humor. It wasn't exactly a grand-slam moment in the history of television, but the audience gave me a good-natured ovation. I felt ridiculous, but hey, I couldn't disappoint Jay Leno.

Appearing on *The Tonight Show* was truly a highlight of the whole World Series experience for me. I watched Johnny Carson as a kid with my dad and then continued when Jay took over. Through the years, *The Tonight Show* has been an icon in the American entertainment culture. I was happy to experience it up close and share our championship with the world.

chapter 9

Heavenly Endings

K-Rod

Frankie Rodriguez

I can still remember the first time I heard about Venezuelan phenom Frankie Rodriguez. Chad Curtis' kid brother, Bill, had played for the Angels in the minor leagues back in the late 1990s. Every time I'd see him, he'd talk about this Latin pitcher on his Class A team named Frankie Rodriguez. He would describe Frankie's pitching abilities as if he were a Greek god sent down to dominate the game of baseball. "He throws 95 miles per hour with the best curveball you will ever see," he'd say. "He's going to be a Hall of Famer!" Always skeptical when I hear superlatives like this, I checked it out with some Angels minor-league staff and they confirmed the evaluation. Could he really be that great? I couldn't wait to see it.

In September 2002, the Angels called up this Rodriguez kid. Not exactly the physical specimen I expected, he was thin and very young-looking. *Well, maybe he'll get a chance to pitch. Then we'll see what he's got against major-league hitters*, I thought to myself. We were in the middle of a late drive for the pennant, though, so it didn't seem to be the ideal opportunity to give the call-ups much work.

The first game in which he pitched was against the A's in Oakland. Earlier in the game I'd had a chance to play catch with him as the bullpen warmed me up in between innings in right field. Not my typical warm-up pitcher, Frankie had the juices pumping, and he threw the first toss about 90 miles per hour. It wasn't the speed that concerned me but the late break that handcuffed me. There was so much cutting movement on the ball that I had to back up a bit to give myself more time to react. *Holy cow,* I thought. *It's absolutely jumping out of his hand!* I had to tell him "*suave,*" so he would take it easy on me.

In the dugout between innings, I told Ersty what had happened. The next inning, he made a point to watch the warm-ups from a distance, and he was equally impressed. That same inning, Scioscia made a pitching change and put Frankie in his first game. Standing in center field with Ersty and G.A., we watched his warm-ups. We were laughing out loud how sick those warm-up pitches looked.

Frankie mowed down the first three A's batters in succession. Every time one of the Oakland hitters swung at a pitch, he missed by a mile. Ersty and I looked at each other with our mouths agape in sheer amazement, as if to say, "Can you believe this guy?" He obviously made the same impression on the coaching staff.

From the very beginning, Frankie was just phenomenal. He lived up to the hype that preceded him. His ability to come up to the big leagues and handle the pressure of a pennant race was amazing, and there's no question that he was a difference-maker for us that October. He was the shot in the arm, the boost we needed to get into the postseason. I'll go so far as to say that without him, I don't think we would have won the World Series. To me, Frankie was the guy who really got us over the hump. He was simply lights-out against everyone he faced. He chewed up all those crucial innings before Percy went in there to close. He was what Mariano Rivera was to closer John Wetteland and the great Yankees teams in the '90s. He was the dominating force that really shortened the game for us.

Whenever I think of Frankie, my mind always goes back to that first day when we played catch in the Oakland outfield. I'm happy to say I was there, warming up what was soon to be the biggest story in baseball, before the world knew about him.

Vladdy

Vladimir Guerrero

There are a handful of players in the game today who truly shine in moments of intense pressure. When the spotlight is on them, they shine like they were born to do it. In the biggest games and against the toughest pitchers, they come through big time. Vladimir Guerrero is a member of that elite club. He takes immense pride in his game and has been a consistent superstar in the major leagues.

The writing was on the wall for me during the 2003 season. My body was really starting to show my age, and I knew the DH role was in my near future. There was a lot of talk about who would replace me in right field. The Angels' intentions were pretty clear when they targeted Vladdy, the top free agent on the market. I was happy to see the team go after a real superstar, and there were never any hurt feelings on my part relinquishing my right-field position.

Vladimir Guerrero's arrival marked the beginning of a new era for the Angels. His bat has helped lead the way to five divisional championships.

When we first got Guerrero, all I heard was that I'd see some of the most amazing things ever I've seen in this game from him. It turns out they hadn't exaggerated. Vladdy's one of the few guys for whom you stop what you're doing and watch when he comes to bat. Who else in the game could you say that about? Barry Bonds, maybe. The second thing people always said about him was what a great teammate he is—and he is, absolutely. Those are two rare things you can't say about every legitimate superstar.

Vladdy lived up to his billing. A statement often heard in the dugout after a typical at-bat might be, "I can't believe he just did that!" Vlad has a knack for doing the unexpected, like swinging at a slider from a left-handed pitcher that might have hit him in the front leg and then golfing it straight down the left-field line for a home run. His ability to do the unexpected makes him a serious threat at the plate, no doubt. But a big misconception some have about him is that he is just a free swinger. Observing him over the years, I can tell you that he's a lot more intelligent at the plate than folks give him credit for. Some go so far as to call him a freak of nature, because of his great hand-eye coordination. Maybe so, but I know from playing with him that every time he steps up to bat he has a definite plan to attack the pitch. He anticipates how pitchers are going to pitch him, and he's good at setting them up.

A great example is Barry Zito. Zito always gave me problems with that big left-handed curve, but Vladdy always just crushed him. I asked him once how he hit him, and what kind of pitches he looked for off of him. His answer surprised me. "I look curveball," he said.

Everybody knows Zito has one of the best curves in the game. Why on earth would you *look* for that pitch, instead of avoiding it and trying to hit the fastball? After I thought about it, though, it occurred to me that there are certain guys about whom you develop a kind of tunnel vision. While Zito's fastballs are never really in a good hitting zone, I was always trying to hit them anyway. His curveball, on the other hand, usually drops in a good spot to hit, but I was always fooled by it because I was looking fastball or change-up.

That was typical Vladdy. The essential difference between Vlad and the rest of us is that where we've probably overanalyzed hitting, he just steps up to the plate and does it. He just has the right frame of mind for success, and to me that's refreshing.

Among the many reasons Vladdy is a such great teammate is that so many Latino players respect and look up to him. He sets a great example for everyone. If the game starts at 7:00 PM, Vladdy's always out there stretching and getting loose at 6:35. Do you think Barry Bonds would ever be caught doing that? I knew he was going to be something special the first day he arrived at camp. It didn't take but a half-hour around the guy to know he was a gamer. You could just sense it. His value to a team is almost immeasurable. His words and actions carry great weight, and his teammates watch and learn from him.

Vlad may not speak English that well, but when he steps up to the plate and swings that bat, there's not an ounce of misunderstanding. He is one heck of a ballplayer.

The One That Got Away

Just about every time I make a public appearance, even though I never played in an actual All-Star Game, I always get introduced as an All-Star. I don't go out of my way to set the record straight, because it really doesn't make much difference at this point. My teammates, peers, and fans recognize that I had a few All-Star–caliber years, and that's good enough for me.

Playing on the West Coast probably didn't help my chances of making the All-Star team, especially during the period when the Angels weren't drawing very well. We were not in a huge media market then, and the Angels were considered the second team in Los Angeles. So when it came to us getting players voted onto the team, we weren't exactly powerhouses at the ballot box. The All-Star team manager filled out his roster by picking players he felt would benefit the team the most, and with guys like Percival, Ersty, and Jimmy Edmonds around—all legitimate All-Stars in their own right—I wasn't about to argue that I belonged at the head of the line.

In all honestly, I was usually so tired by the All-Star break that I welcomed the three or four days off with my family. Maybe it would have been nice to have played in the midsummer classic at least once, if only to experience all the excitement surrounding the event, but I've never lost any sleep or doubted my credentials as a ballplayer because it isn't on my résumé. I knew what my capabilities were, and so did my peers. Besides, the West Coast media always griped about me not making the team, which was always nice to hear.

After we won the World Series in 2002, there was talk that 2003 would be my opportunity to make the All-Star team. The World Series managers are always picked to manage the next year's game. That meant after the fans selected the starting lineups, Sosh would be filling out the rest of the American League roster with his picks to best shape the team. In the past, some managers had shown loyalties to their own players at times. It was a natural for everyone to think this might be my best opportunity.

As the season progressed, my play didn't attract the attention typical for All-Star consideration. As the game approached, there were a lot of difficult questions being asked of Sosh and myself: would he use a roster spot on an undeserving player like me?

The game actually means something now, with home-field advantages in the World Series at stake, so the days of filling spots out of loyalty were over. There were so many deserving players out there, that my selection just wasn't justified. Sosh chose someone else for the spot and he absolutely made the correct decision.

In my career, I should have made at least one All-Star Game for sure, but 2003 wasn't the one. To make an exception for me would have been an injustice to someone more deserving, not to mention the American League. In my prime years, I believe that my play stacks up against anyone's. Fair or not, that is the system I played under, and I'm okay with it. My prime years had come and gone. Besides, I have something that 95 percent of all those All-Stars only wish they had: a World Series ring. If I had to choose between that and being an All-Star, it would be no contest. I'd grab for the gold ring and never look back.

The Steroid Era

The first time I heard about steroids was years ago, when I was in high school. It was during football season, so I was spending a lot of time inside the weight room. But it was my baseball coach who pulled me off to the side for a talk. From out of the blue, he turned his discussion to the harmful effects of steroids. He implored me to exercise caution and good judgment if I was exposed to them.

Caught a little off guard by his suspicious tone, I couldn't help but be a little defensive. *Does he assume I'm on steroids because I play football and spend a lot of time lifting weights?* My long hours in the weight room had cast a shadow of suspicion on me. I barely knew anything about steroids and certainly hadn't come into contact with them. I had just turned 16 that summer, and going into my junior year I came back to school almost six inches taller and about 25 pounds heavier. Puberty kicking in, combined with my weight-training work, caused a change in my appearance that was dramatic.

Looking back, I realize that my coach had a difficult task in trying to protect me and others from the negative influences out there. I am grateful for his concern and for taking time to explain the harmful effects of steroids to me.

Whenever I speak at an event, the topic of steroids is invariably the most popular subject matter. Performance enhancing drugs (PEDs) such as steroids and human growth hormone (HGH) came onto the scene during the peak years of my career. I suppose any book written by a player from my generation is faced with addressing the issue. It's tough to have played in an era that has so much suspicion and speculation surrounding it. I would like to think that the majority of players were clean, but clearly some aspects of the game changed. Sure, there might have been some whispers along the way, but I guess that most of us were in denial that it was as big of a problem as it turned out to be.

Looking back, I suppose there were telltale signs along the way—home-run records being broken, middle relievers unexpectedly throwing the ball three miles per hour harder, or average utility players suddenly hitting more home runs than they ever had before. At the time, though, we looked at these spikes in performance and rationalized, "That's just a juiced ball." Now, of course, we know it wasn't the ball that was juiced. It was tough to understand to what extent the game was being influenced by PEDs. Was it just the big power hitters? How could it possibly help a pitcher? Of course, new revelations have slowly emerged, revealing that it wasn't just hitters but pitchers, too.   And young guys, old guys, MVPs, and bench players. PEDs weren't just limited to a few players or even a particular segment of players. Everyone who used them saw a benefit in his performance. It raised the level of play on the field, making it more and more difficult for those who chose not to use them.

Today, I have a better understanding of why the threshold for determining power hitters changed during the middle of my career. When I first came up to the big leagues, if a player hit 30 homers and drove in 100 runs he was labeled a power hitter and ended up one of the top 10 hitters in the league. I fell into that category my rookie year and continued to perform at that level during the bulk of my healthy playing days. I always prided myself on taking care of my body by getting my rest and sticking to a weight-lifting program both in and out of season. This was "performance enhancement" as I understood it, and it paid off for me. Something began to change, though, in the late '90s. I kept up my typical production, but I was moving *down* the list of top hitters instead of toward the top. Typical power-hitter numbers of the past couldn't even land you in the top 10 anymore! That bar was raised from 30 to more than 40 home runs over a short period of time. On the top end, there were guys hitting 50, 60, and in 2001, a new record of 73 home runs. A major-league record that had stood for over 50 years was suddenly broken by three different players in a five-year span.

I began to rationalize that my own decline was due to some of the injuries I had developed. So when I started feeling healthy, I always wondered why I wasn't benefiting from the so-called "juiced ball" that people talked about. It didn't seem to be going any farther for me—actually, it was becoming more difficult for me to do what I was accustomed to doing in the game. My perceived lack of production started to take a toll on me mentally. In 2001, after my first shoulder surgery, my drop off in production almost put me over the edge. Now, I realize I was fighting more than just myself. The playing field was becoming increasingly unbalanced for those who tried to play it the right way.

Looking back at the late '90s you can see that it was a new era of competitive advantages and rewards. The growth of the game raised the financial stakes to astronomical heights for those that could separate themselves from the pack. The financial incentive outweighed the risk of any potential side effects from PEDs. Like anything else in society, the lust for fame and fortune trumped what was legal, moral, and healthy. For some players, it was too tempting an opportunity to pass up.

Of course, I realize that as long as baseball has been around, there have always been those who have found a way to take advantage of the system and not get caught. But corked bats and pitchers using foreign substances and scuffing the ball were pretty much the extent of what constituted cheating. I believe that using steroids goes way beyond those other forms of cheating. Steroids made players become more than nature intended them to be, dramatically elevating their performance level. It created an unhealthy culture in the game that screamed, "Get on the program or get left behind!" It was a perfect storm for abuse, and Major League Baseball, as well as the rest of the world, got blindsided. Who could have anticipated the bodybuilding phenomenon, fueled by steroid use, would manifest itself in professional baseball?

I have always been determined to never compromise my faith or my principles. I always relied on my God-given talent when I took the field. So the idea of using PEDs to enhance my performance was a line I chose not to cross. As I became more aware of the problem of steroid use, I discovered that for some players it wasn't all black and white. Some of them were guys I respected on and off the field, players who were truly faced with career-jeopardizing decisions. To them, it wasn't about becoming the league MVP or signing a huge free-agent contract. It was about trying to keep a job when you know your competition is on the juice because you've endured a career-threatening arm injury, or simply trying to stay in the lineup while hurt in order to fulfill your contract obligation. I would never make a blanket statement about steroid use. But to truly comprehend the difficult moral and ethical decisions these guys struggled with, I guess you have to put yourself in their shoes. It's easy to condemn steroids, but the pressure to perform at a consistently high level is tremendous. Faced with losing the job, I can better understand their rationalization.

The game seemed to change overnight in the steroid era. I can understand the baseball purist leading the charge for the past legends of the game. There has been talk about changing the record books and putting asterisks next to some players' names. I wouldn't endorse it. I don't think there are any realistic answers for dealing with the inflated numbers of this era. Where can you draw the line of certainty? We will never know. As names continue to come out, it will be up to the fans to determine the historical significance of each player's production during this time.

In the future I am confident the game on the field will return to normal levels of play. The hard lessons learned through the so-called steroid era have developed new measures for testing and have raised public awareness as to the dangers of the drugs. Our national pastime is in a much better place today to protect the long-term interests and health of its players and the game. But, like many of you, I have to wonder: On a level playing field, where do the great players of my era stack up against the history of the game? Are they even superstars without steroids? We may never know. One thing I do know is this: My 299 home runs don't compare much with the great home-run hitters of the game, but I'm proud of each and every one of them.

The Tim Salmon Foundation

Being a major-league player is a tremendous honor. The platform we are given can be used for a lot of good. The opportunity to make an impact in the community around me was one of the most gratifying things I had during my playing career. As a father of four children, raising and shaping their dreams is very rewarding. Through community involvement I realized that there are a lot of children who don't have the same advantages mine do. To know that there are children out there who don't have love, support, and stability from their parents just breaks my heart.

Marci and I were led to work with disadvantaged youth early in my career, and we decided to focus our community-service efforts with them. We developed a directed approach toward the community in which we lived. Our intention was to go beyond the typical player involvement of making an appearance and writing a check. We wanted something we could experience as a family, something Marci and the kids could get behind when I was on the road.

We settled on two charities: Family Solutions and Laurel House. Family Solutions has since merged with Canyon Acres and is a foster-care agency that provides group homes, care treatment, and supportive services for foster children in Orange County. Laurel House is a temporary shelter that provides similar services for teens in crisis. Established in a normal neighborhood (and down the street from where I lived) Laurel House provided short-term housing and counseling for teenagers who need a break from their environment. Housing six kids at a time, surrogate guardians look after the kids, providing them whatever support and treatment they need to get back on track.

My family has had a great relationship with these two organizations over the years and have gotten to know the children serviced. We've had the kids over for barbecues, taken them out to dinner, provided tickets to Angels games and Disneyland, and most important, given the organizations the resources they need to provide healthy environments for the kids. For over 12 years now, the Tim Salmon Golf Classic has raised funds critical to the operation of these two facilities. I am so proud of the efforts that so many people in Orange County have made to partner with us. Without a doubt, the best part of doing charity work is seeing a community come together to meet the needs of the less fortunate.

In addition to these two charities, my foundation also established the "Fishbowl" out in the right-field stands at the stadium. It is a reserved section of 100 seats designated for all Orange County charities involved with youth services. For every home stand we passed out hundreds of free tickets to different charities, and over the years thousands of kids who might not otherwise have seen a major-league ballgame have benefited from the program.

For years my passion was baseball, and I was fortunate to live out my dreams. Now I want to be around to help my own kids, as well as other kids in need, develop their own passions and live out their own dreams. It's also good for my own children to see that life is not just about their needs but also what you can do to help others. I am thankful for the baseball platform I was given and the opportunities it provided to make a difference in the community.

The Last Run

There is a season for everything in life, and sometimes when seasons change, moving on can be challenging. My body's ability to play baseball began to change during the 2001 season. For the first time in my life I was faced with the realization of my own baseball mortality. I was slowing down. Playing the game required more physical and mental preparation than I had needed before. It got to the point where I was putting in more time in the trainer's room preparing for the game than I spent on the field. It is a stark realization for all players when that day arrives.

I ground it out through the next few years, and I was rewarded with a world championship in 2002. That made the struggle worthwhile, but when my body began to beg for mercy in 2004, I knew retirement was a wise consideration. I ended up missing half of the '04 season and all of '05 due to surgery to repair my ailing shoulder and knee. It was a bitter pill to swallow, knowing my playing days were most likely over. There is no way to prepare for having something you've poured your whole life into, an entire career, come to an end. It wasn't exactly the ride off into the sunset I always imagined it would be. But I remember Gary DiSarcina always saying that 99 percent of players never go out on their own terms.

It wasn't how I wanted it to end, but with a grueling 18 months of rehab ahead of me, I conceded that it was probably over. For me there was a certain amount of relief in the realization that I wouldn't have to put my body through the torment of a season's worth of games again. I also knew that I had only one chance to rehab these surgically repaired injuries, so I bit the bullet one last time and put everything I had into my rehabilitation. It turned out it was every bit as hard as playing the game itself.

My goal in rehab was to come out on the other end still able to play golf and have an active lifestyle with my kids. Still, and maybe because I knew no other way, I approached the rehab with the intent of any other player trying to get back on the field. It ended up being terribly taxing, both physically and mentally. There were plenty of days when I thought I would never swing anything again, let alone get back in baseball-playing shape. Everyone told me it would take 10 to 12 months to "turn the corner," and they were right. The healing process crept at a snail's pace.

Then one day I finally had a glimmer of hope. I took some dry swings with a bat and realized for the first time in years I could swing it without the sharp pain I had grown so accustomed to feeling. Was it possible that I might be able to swing a bat like in my days of old? I came away from that day so encouraged that I began to think the impossible. Maybe I could come back and play the game I used to love and have a chance to go out on my own terms.

Adding fuel to my rehab efforts was how easily the game had moved on without me. That too, is another depressing realization for players. These sentiments combined with my renewed encouragement motivated me like never before. I was coming to spring training, yes, but it to make the roster, not to retire. That became my new goal. It was just a matter of whether or not my body would continue to respond to the treatments.

That fall, I hit the batting cage for the first time and was pleasantly surprised. My shoulder felt great, but my troublesome knee was still iffy. The doctors injected my knee with SYNVISC, a natural lubricant thought to help with arthritic knees. When I arrived in camp, my knee was the only looming question on my mind. If it could hold up, I thought I had a chance. The bigger question was now for my family: were they ready to give me back to the game?

Being home for the past year and a half had given us a glimpse of what retirement would look like, and from that side, it was all good. I started coaching the kids' teams, going on field trips, and taking family vacations during the summer. We never really considered going back to that baseball lifestyle again. It was a lot to ask of them to be prepared to live with the answer. I think it helped that I was at the end of my career; healthy or not, I would be finished in a year or two anyway.

The Angels brought me into camp acknowledging that even if I was healthy, chances were very slim that they would have a roster spot for me. Everyone agreed that if I had to retire, it would be in my best interests to do so in an Angels uniform. I couldn't have agreed more. As fate would have it, a couple injuries to some key players had opened the door for me to stay where my heart was, and my knee responded decently, allowing me to show everyone I was back.

That year, spring training was much different than any other I had experienced in the past. I came in trying to make a team, and for the first time in my career, I had to earn it. The pressure to perform under the circumstances required an in-season focus from the first day of camp. It was a strange feeling to be on the outside looking in. Watching G.A., Vlad, Figgy, and the rest of them ease into their games, I realized that wasn't a luxury I had anymore. In all those years on the other side, I had never contemplated what the guys in my shoes were experiencing. It would be the first of many new revelations for me that season.

I actually had a pretty good spring. It helped that, with the newly formed World Baseball Classic, a few of our Latin players were gone for a couple weeks representing their respective countries. Their absence gave some much-needed at-bats. As we neared the end of camp, I knew I was on the short list of players vying for those last couple roster spots. Mickey Hatcher told me that everyone was pulling for me and they just hoped everything would fall into place. Then we broke camp for Anaheim to play the Dodgers in the "Freeway Series." It was surreal to know that everything hung in the balance of the next 48 hours. I had come all this way, and I still didn't know for sure what lay ahead.

The game against the Dodgers that night gave me a view of what my future would be if I made the roster. All the starters were back, which meant I had to wait around for a pinch-hit appearance later in the game. I wasn't sure if I was capable of being a bench player. I answered that question for Sosh in the seventh inning, when I pinch hit a home run off the bench. Now that wasn't so hard!

I found out the next day that I had made the roster as the 24th or 25th guy—not too shabby considering all I had been through in the last 18 months. I was heading back to Anaheim to stay.

Opening Day was truly special. I don't think anyone—including me—expected to see me on the third-base line during introductions. It was gratifying to be back in whatever capacity I could be. The season opened for us with a few of our guys still banged up, so I had an opportunity to play. I was happy to be on the field again and performing at a level I remembered before my injuries. I was contributing to the winning cause, and I felt right at home. Surprisingly, I found myself back in the heart of the order doing what I do best, working the count and putting together tough at-bats.

Playing about five days a week was a little more than anyone expected. I did have some lingering concerns about whether or not my knee could handle the day-to-day rigors. When the guys they initially were counting on got healthy, my role settled back into that of a bench player. In my limited playing time, I hit .265 with nine home runs and 27 RBI. I was hoping my efforts might help the Angels get back to the postseason, but it wasn't in the cards.

As the season wound down and our playoff hopes vanished, all the attention turned toward my impending retirement. I was nearing the coveted 300-home-run mark and with a week to play, I started getting more at-bats. I hit my 299th home run on the last Wednesday night game of the season. As much as I tried to hit a home run in the final four games, I just couldn't do it.

During the final homestand of the regular season, the Angels honored me with between-inning tributes highlighting my career.

The last game of the season was decreed "Tim Salmon Day." The fanfare included a 10-minute highlight video of my career and about a half-dozen standing ovations. The grounds crew had even mowed my name and No. 15 into the outfield grass. It was a wonderful gesture on behalf of the organization and meant a lot to my family and friends. But it was also very uncomfortable for me. At the time, a special day celebrating only me made me squirm.

We played Oakland that day, and several of the A's players congratulated me. They seemed pretty impressed with the sendoff. Hearing that from them made me feel good that I had gone about things the right away. The way I played the game ultimately gave me the respect of my fellow peers. From the very beginning, that's what I'd wanted. The guys I always looked up to, like Chili Davis, Cal Ripken Jr., and Andre Dawson, had made an impact on my career—and people noticed. I worked hard, stayed out of trouble, and followed the lead of others. All in all, I was blessed to have a wonderful career.

In my final season, I dedicated my play to my recently departed friend, former team chaplain Chuck Obremski. Chuck's battle with cancer gave him a platform to live out his favorite Bible verse, 2 Timothy 4:7. It reads, "I have fought the good fight, I have finished the race, I have kept the faith." Stepping onto the field for the last time, the significance of this verse rang true in my heart. I gave everything I had to the game and more. It was a journey during which I depended on God every step of the way, and He didn't disappoint.

The days leading up to my last game were humbling to say the least. At every at-bat, I was given a standing ovation. Everyone was pulling for me to hit one more home run to get to 300. The last game became somewhat emotional for me. I was aware that these were my last at-bats forever. The finality was sinking in.

I was probably trying to do too much, but things just weren't going well for me at the plate in that last game. After a walk and a

couple pop-outs, I just wasn't feeling it. We rallied late to tie the game in the bottom of the eighth inning. With runners on second and third and less than two outs, I came to bat with a chance to win the game. My last at-bat was shaping up to be a classic one to end on. *What a way to go out*, I remember thinking. The crowd was on their feet. Swinging at the first pitch, an inside fastball, I popped up to the shortstop. I couldn't believe it. As soon as it came off my bat, I reacted with disgust. Aside from all the sentimental reasons for getting a hit, I really wanted to be the hero one last time. There it was: no game-winning hit, no home run, just a lousy pop-up.

To say I that was mad is an understatement. As I stormed back to the dugout, the crowd got my attention by giving me a standing ovation. I definitely was not in the right mood to fully appreciate it, but I gave them a wave of acknowledgement and ducked back into the dugout. Slamming my bat into the bat rack one last time, I noticed the crowed continued to cheer, signaling for a curtain call. Then it struck me, the irony of the situation. This was a curtain call requested for a player failing to get the job done. Immediately it reminded me of something all too familiar to those of us who are Christians. God used the moment to remind me of His grace and mercy! The fans were bestowing on me the same thing God does for us as Christians. How many times have we all fallen on our faces trying to follow Jesus, yet God picks us back up and offers His grace and mercy? It wasn't about that last at-bat or one more win for the fans. It was appreciation for the cumulative effort I had made for so many years.

In that moment I was reminded how blessed my career had been. I had so much for which to be thankful. It's amazing how this one moment spoke volumes to me. This chapter of my life ended perfectly as I relied one last time on God's eternal teaching to finish strong in the faith. Am I disappointed that I didn't get to 300 home runs? No. 299 always makes for a better story.

If I Had a Nickel...

If I had a nickel for every time somebody asked what I'm doing now, I'd probably have more money than I did when I played. The answer to that question is, I'm doing all the things I dreamed about doing for the last 20 years. Coaching the kids' football and baseball teams, going on ski trips, hunting, surfing, traveling around the world with my family, and trying my hand at some business ventures is more than enough to keep me busy.

Do I miss playing baseball? A little bit. Whenever I watch a game or visit the clubhouse, I get those longing feelings. Still, I can rest easy

Saying good-bye was made a whole lot easier having the warmth and support of the fans. Photo courtesy of Getty Images

Photo courtesy of the author

in retirement with the satisfaction of where I am and what I was able to accomplish. As a player I had it all: the long career, big contracts, a World Series championship, fan appreciation, and the unique connection of playing with only one organization. What else could a player ask for? If you asked a 12-year-old kid on a sandlot today to describe his big-league dream, he couldn't paint a picture any better than the one I experienced.

Having time on my hands allows me to give some of it back to the community in a variety of charitable ways. My golf tournament, held every year at Coto de Caza, has opened the door to many new relationships with like-minded people looking to make positive changes in their communities. In 2008 I had a great opportunity to visit our American combat troops in Afghanistan on a goodwill mission. For 10 days, Jeff Nelson, Dean Palmer, Mike Remlinger, and I flew around the country bringing a little "back home" to the troops. Seeing the American military machine in action is impressive. The opportunity to talk with the troops and boost the morale of the men and women defending freedom was something I'll never forget. Their response to us was overwhelming. Baseball means a lot to our troops over there, because it gives them a chance to get away from the desert for a while, at least in their minds.

Being in Afghanistan really put life into perspective for me. A lot of the soldiers would approach me and ask me why I retired. I'd tell them that I got tired of the travel, or that my body hurt too much— and then realized I was talking to guys who hadn't seen their families for 18 months, and some faced the prospect of death every day. Wow, did I feel like a heel. As a player I got to go home at least every two weeks, and if I got hurt too bad, I'd get a two-week vacation on the DL. All of us on the trip realized pretty fast that we needed to come up with a different answer—that is, if we didn't want to get hog-tied and thrown onto the next transport back to the States.

My last day as a player was a special one that I was blessed to share with my family. Photo courtesy of the author

One of the most fulfilling things I've done since I left baseball is that I went back to college and completed my degree. Not finishing college had always bothered me, so I returned and earned my Bachelor's degree in applied management. It took me 20 years to get my diploma, and what made it extra special was having my kids in the stands watching. I always tell them that education is such an important part of their lives. In the last two years, my kids watched Dad put his money where his mouth is, doing homework every night and writing a ton of papers. For them to see my efforts rewarded when I took that walk across the stage with 600 other graduates was a very proud day for all of us.

As far as professional baseball is concerned, I'm not out of it entirely. In the last few seasons I've had the privilege to attend the Angels' spring training as a guest coach. Sitting in on Mike Scioscia's morning meetings with the staff has been a great learning experience. Seeing how the game plan unfolds and knowing the effort that goes into running a team is eye-opening. Like just about everything else in society, there's much more micromanaging these days. For Mike Scioscia, it's not just the big club he's concerned with but the entire minor leagues as well. Sitting in on meetings, I get to see a very clear road map from point *A* to *B*.

Being a part of spring training in this capacity has definitely rekindled a spark for the game at the professional level. The greatest challenge for me returning in some coaching capacity at the professional level is my family. My No. 1 priority is the needs of my kids, especially at such an important time in their development. I want to be around for my kids and help them develop their own passions in life. Now, if an arrangement could be worked out that allowed me to do both, then I would definitely consider it. For the time being, though, I'll just watch the Angels from a distance, wish them the best, and thank God daily for blessing me the way he did.

Speaking Circuit

When I am out speaking, often I am asked questions like, "Who were your best friends on the team?"

"What does your typical day look like in the big leagues?"

"What is it like traveling on a charter jet?"

"How do you avoid the temptations on the road?"

"What's your favorite stadium to play in?"

These are all great questions that really give the fans great insight into the life of a major-leaguer. When I think of other high-profile professions, like being a rock star, I find myself wondering some of the same basic things, so I can understand the intrigue about the lifestyle behind being famous.

I've been fortunate to have some great relationships while I played with the Angels. Being in one place for so long meant that friends came and went over the course of my career. Chad Curtis and Damion Easley were my close friends early on, up until 1995. In 1995 we got a pitcher named Shawn Boskie whom I knew from my off-season workouts. He left a few years later, about the time Orlando Palmeiro established himself with the big club. Orlando was my closest friend for about five or six years until he left the Angels in 2003.

In 2001, David Eckstein came on board with the team, and we seemed to hit it off pretty well. He left us after the 2004 season, about the time Robb Quinlan started his tenure.

Friendships come and go, in baseball and in life, but there was one individual from my baseball life who will always be important to me. My friendship with G.A. over the years has been a great one. He doesn't open up to too many people, so I count it an honor to know him like I do. For the most part my relationships with these guys was based upon similar interests both on and off the field. Good character, faith, and family values are the bonds that strengthened our relationships. I am so thankful for them because they kept me grounded over the years and focused on the right things.

Most fans are surprised when they realize what the baseball schedule requires. Its not just showing up at game time and playing a few times a week. The season starts in mid-February and continues every day until the first of October. And that's if you *don't* make the playoffs. Off-days consist mainly of travel, getting to the next city to start a new series. In a typical season, the schedule might show close to 20 days off. As a West Coast team, the Angels spend about 17 of those in transit. Maybe once or twice a season we get a day at home with the family. It's a grind, for sure, and that is why players are so protective of their time off with their families.

A typical game-day routine at home would go something like this:

10:00 AM: Eat breakfast

10:30 AM: Spend time with the family around the house

1:00 PM: Lunch

1:30 PM: Take a short nap

2:30 PM: Drive to the stadium

3:00 PM: Arrive and dress for workouts

3:15 PM: Start daily pregame routine including any maintenance issues, video scouting, or extra work on the field

4:30 PM: Team stretch

4:45 PM: Batting practice

5:30 PM: Change out of "wet" clothes and get something to eat

6:00 PM: Team meetings at 6:00, if needed

6:30 PM: Get dressed

6:45 PM: Pre-game stretching on the field

7:00 PM: On the top step for the National Anthem

7:05 PM: First pitch

When the game ended, I'd get 20 minutes of icing in the training room, do any postgame interviews, hit the shower, and grab some dinner from the spread room. I'd head home around 11:30, and after an hour or so to wind down, I tried to be in bed by 12:30

or 1:00 AM, hopefully sleep well, and start the process all over again the next day. Such is the life of a major league baseball player. It was a routine that didn't allow for much variation.

During my first couple years in the big leagues, I really enjoyed traveling on the road. Traveling in the big leagues is first-class all the way, especially after all the bus rides in the minors. Everything from the meal money allowance, to charted buses that drove up to chartered planes on the tarmac, to the luxury hotels in which we stayed. It was all top-notch. The events of 9/11 changed some of those travel conveniences, but we still traveled like rock stars. There is a celebrity vibe associated with a professional team that attracts the public's attention in each city. In New York for instance, just walking down the street people recognize you and are sure to remind you about your fate later that night.

After seeing all the attractions the cities had to offer after a few years, I didn't enjoy the travel as much. Having a young family at home always made for long good-byes. I think most players would agree that the hardest part of baseball is being away from family.

When I traveled on the road, the nightlife never appealed to me. I might meet up with a few guys and play some cards back in the hotel, but I was never one to hit the streets. As a faithfully married man, I was always careful to protect my commitment to my wife. I think the situations you make available to yourself dictate the actions that follow. Always having a like-minded teammate to pal around with insulated me from many of the temptations that persist. Just as important is the fact that I was always in bed at a decent hour to get the rest my body desperately needed to play the next day. As much as my body broke down later in my career, an active nightlife would have shortened my career even more.

People always ask me what my favorite stadium to play in was. Answering that is akin to asking "Which of your kids do you like the best?" It's the big leagues; every stadium is pretty awesome. It would be easier to say which ones I hate, but, here is my short list of favorites. Outside of the Big A, Yankee Stadium has to be on the top of the list because it's where I made my debut. I like Fenway because of the Green Monster, the old Tiger Stadium for the history, Camden Yards and Jacobs Field for their modern structures, and I like the Ballpark in Arlington because I always hit well there. What field do I hate the most? Probably Oakland Alameda—but only because we played so many day games there. It was always so bright on the eyes!

Retirement has given me many opportunities to share my stories and insight behind the game. I really do enjoy the fan interaction. All I have are memories of great experiences, so any time someone wants to hear about them, I'm usually available to tell them.

Epilogue

My last few seasons under Arte Moreno were among the best of my career. Like Gene Autry, Mr. Moreno is hands-on and player-friendly. He's a huge fan of the game, and he wants to win in the worst way. Whatever you need to win, if you can justify it, he will do it. From a player's perspective, the knowledge that your owner will do anything it takes to win is exhilarating. He has earned the players' and the fans' respect. Playing in front of packed houses every night is evidence of that.

Something that will always stand out in my memory is that first day I signed an Angels contract. I went to Gene Autry Park in Mesa, Arizona. All of the players were seated on the outfield grass around Joe Maddon and the coaches and Joe told us. "You guys have got to believe you're the core that turns this organization around and gives it its first championship!"

To have been a part of that group that did exactly as Joe predicted is tremendously gratifying. Not only do we have a championship trophy, but we are also a team the community is proud to claim. The prospects for the Angels organization couldn't be better. Under the helm of terrific ownership, a knowledgeable front office, unbelievable scouting, and a great manager running the ship, the Angels should always be a playoff contender. Winning another world championship is a lot harder than people realize, because so many things have to

Arte Moreno is the one responsible for elevating the Angels to the elite franchise they are today. His player-friendly approach and commitment to winning is welcomed by all who play for him.

happen just right. I know the Angels have been close the last few years only to get knocked off, but someday it will happen again. The Angels are primed to win another championship soon.

I'm proud to have had the opportunity to come back and play in my childhood hometown. Although I had always dreamed it would be for the Dodgers, I couldn't be happier that it was with the Angels. No longer the stepchild in Los Angeles, the Angels finally have the respect and the following in Southern California. I was lucky to be a part of that sea change, something that has impacted a lot of people's lives. It's only going to get better in the days ahead.

Acknowledgments

Rob Goldman and Tim Salmon would like to thank the following:
Tom Bast and Michael Emmerich at Triumph Books for taking on the project, Adam Motin for your guidance, and Katy Sprinkel for your editing skills. Tim Mead, Angels vice-president of communications, for your friendship and support. Special thanks to Angels communication manager Eric Kay for your professionalism and photos.

Pete Ehrmann: your editing skills were a big key to this project. We appreciate your diligence and hard work.

To Joe Maddon, for your foreword and insights.

Tim Salmon would like to thank the following:
My Lord and Savior Jesus Christ for blessing me with the ability to play baseball in the major leagues.

Marci, the ultimate baseball wife, and Callie, Jacob, Katelyn, and Ryan, for giving me the right perspective on life's journey. My mom and dad for their continued love and support through the years. And Mike, for sharpening my athletic skills in those early years like only a brother could. The prayers from the Husteads and my extended family of friends at SBC kept me grounded in my faith.

Ted Blake, John Pierson, Ed Wolf, Gil Stafford, Donny Long, Nate Oliver, Gene Richards, Lenny Sakata, Max Oliveras, Bruce Hines, Joe Maddon, Chili Davis, Rod Carew, Larry Bowa, George

Hendrick, Sam Suplizio, Ron Roenicke, Mickey Hatcher, and Mike Scioscia for teaching me how to play the game. Chad Curtis, Damion Easley, Shawn Boskie, Orlando Palmiero, and Garret Anderson for being friends to hang with on all those road trips. And to all my teammates through the years who put up with Timmy Land!

Ned Bergert, Rick Smith, Adam Nevila, Dr. Craig Milhouse, and Dr. Lewis Yocum for doing whatever it took to keep me on the field. Ken Higdon and his clubhouse staff over the years, Keith, Corey, Shane, Stevie, and Mikey, for keeping my life in order at the stadium.

The Autrys, Disney, and the Morenos for making the Angels such a great organization to play for.

Finally, to Rob Goldman, whose love for the great Angels tradition encouraged me to share with him my journey.

Rob Goldman would like to thank the following:
Jon Madian and Marshall Terrill. The Wallens—Bob, Betty, Billy, Cassy, Mitch, Marcus, and Riley—for keeping the home fires burning. The Kendalls—Sally, Mike, Amy, Greg, and especially Kevin—for the nuggets and good times. Joey Cooperman, Tom Duino, and Jim Doss for your technical help, proofreading and photos.

Larry Babcock, Rob Basom, Charlie Baker, John Carpino, Geoff Bennett, the Conejo Angels, Jerry Frizzel, Bill Gifford, Brian Harkins, Jen Hoyer, Rex Hudler, Matt Hutchison, JT Jara, Liz, Nancy Mazmanian, Mike Obremski, Troy Percival, Rich Rice, Chuck Richter at angelswin.com, Bob Rogers, Mike Scioscia, Bill Shaikin, Mike Salmon, Marci Salmon, Rick Smith, Scott Smith, Brad Sturz, Steven Travers, Doug Ward, Hector "H" Vasquez, Rick Vaughn, Vince Willet, Chris, and Dave: Your contributions are greatly appreciated.

Finally, to Tim Salmon: thanks for trusting me with your story. I appreciate the sacrifices you made in getting it done. It was a marathon, but I truly enjoyed the experience and your company.